GAMES
WITH CODES & CIPHERS

NORVIN PALLAS

DOVER PUBLICATIONS, INC.
Mineola, New York

Dedicated to Ricky, Shawn, Mark, and Joey

Bibliographical Note

This Dover edition, first published in 2019, is an unabridged
republication of the second printing (1972) of *Code Games*,
copublished by Sterling Publishing Co., Inc., New York, and Oak
Tree Press Co., Ltd., London, in 1971.

Library of Congress Cataloging-in-Publication Data

Names: Pallas, Norvin, author.
Title: Games with codes and ciphers / Norvin Pallas.
Other titles: Code games
Description: Mineola, New York: Dover Publications, Inc., 2019. |
    Originally published: Code games. New York: Sterling Pub.
    Co., 1971.
Identifiers: LCCN 2019008956| ISBN 9780486838465 | ISBN
    0486838463
Subjects: LCSH: Ciphers—Juvenile literature.
Classification: LCC Z103.3 .P35 2019 | DDC 652/.8—dc23
LC record available at https://lccn.loc.gov/2019008956

Manufactured in the United States by LSC Communications
83846301   2019
www.doverpublications.com

CONTENTS

INTRODUCTION

What for?

For fun.

It is true that every large nation spends many millions of dollars each year protecting its own communications and trying to break down the communications of other nations, even those that are "friends." Because this activity is highly secret, it undoubtedly covers up many blunders, much waste, and perhaps outright immorality. Much of this cloak-and-dagger business seems to resemble the actions of small boys going to great ends to accomplish nothing except to fulfill some private fantasy. One wonders if much of this information, coming in by the carload, might not be gathered more simply, cheaply, and reliably by open methods.

But we are in it for fun. Cryptography, writing in code and cipher, represents a most happy blend of language and mathematics. It obviously deals in language, yet it deals with it in a mathematical way.

Like many of my generation (and, I sincerely trust, like many children of today), my enthusiasm for cryptography was first aroused by the Sherlock Holmes stories. Who can dismiss the unforgettable *Adventure of the Dancing Men*? It is true that this concerned a simple substitution cipher that any amateur can learn to break, but it had the added gimmicks of disguise, and a flag in a doll's hand to denote the end of a word. Holmes's decipherment was delightful to a youngster, and Conan Doyle's order of letter frequencies, E T A O I N S H R D L, turned out to be very similar to a table I developed for myself. Then I recognized that strange printer's error, *etaoin shrdlu*, which occasionally gets into a newspaper by accident.

It occurs when the printer, having made an error, completes the line by running his finger vertically down the keys with the intention of discarding that particular line.

But there was one sentence in the story which intrigued me. Holmes states he is fairly familiar with all forms of secret writings, and is the author of a trifling monograph upon the subject in which he analyzes 160 separate ciphers. I set out to discover Holmes's 160 systems. I learned that there were hardly a dozen basic systems, but if the possible variations and combinations are counted, the number becomes virtually unlimited. What were Holmes's 160 systems? I never found them.

My real pleasure came about when I discovered that I, too, could break simple substitution ciphers, just the way Sherlock Holmes did. I even found that sometimes I could read messages with nothing more than a dash for each letter with the proper breaks between words, if I had some idea what the other person was thinking about at the moment (– –– –––––– ––––– might be "I am going home"). Naturally this led me to devise more difficult ciphers and then to try my hand at breaking them as well. There was even that exciting moment when I broke my first Playfair cipher—and lightning promptly struck the tree outside my window! What this portended, if anything, I do not know.

To be more serious, let me remind you of what President Harding once said: "Gentlemen do not read each other's mail." He was speaking of gentleman nations, of course. Obviously, we do not live in this kind of world. But it is something to think about and to work toward.

A SIMPLE THING TO REMEMBER

Nearly everyone is familiar with simple substitution messages. An alphabet table is drawn up and each letter of the new alphabet is substituted for one of the letters of the real alphabet. Sometimes numbers or symbols are used instead of letters to seem more mysterious, but this really does not make the code more difficult.

For the simplest table, write half the alphabet—in any order—on the top line, and the other half on the bottom line:

E A N R H L WF G P V X Q
T O I S D MU C Y B K J Z

To write the message, "Was he held back?" exchange each letter for the one directly above or below it:

W A S H E H E L D B A C K
U O R D T D T M H P O F V

This is a back-and-forth, or reciprocal, system. The message is decoded exactly the same way it is written.

Here is a non-reciprocal alphabet table:

A B C D E F G H I J K L M N O P Q R S T U V W X Y Z
L M U Z P D K F V B X O R J T I Y A C H N S Q G E W

The same message would be written:

W A S H E H E L D B A C K
Q L C F P F P O Z ML U X

This message is a little more difficult to read. You must find each letter on the bottom line of the substitution table and substitute the letter *above*.

But suppose you made a mistake. Suppose you received the

above message and tried to read it by finding each letter on the *top* line and substituting the letter beneath. What would you get? Try it and see:

QL C F P F P O Z ML U X
– – – – – – – – – – – – –

Remember that a code is like a lock. You turn the key one way to lock it and the opposite way to open it. In decoding a non-reciprocal alphabet table, keep in mind that you must find the letters in the code on the *bottom* line, and translate them into the regular alphabet on the *top* line.

WHY JOHNNY HAD TO STAY AFTER SCHOOL

"What are you doing, Johnny? This is supposed to be a study hour." Miss Jewel's voice was very sharp.

Johnny tried to slip some papers under his huge geography book, but the teacher caught him.

"Bring those papers up to my desk." Johnny obeyed reluctantly, and Miss Jewel looked them over.

"It's a kind of code," Johnny explained.

"So I guessed," said Miss Jewel acidly. "Well, since you've managed to disrupt our study period, perhaps our class will be interested in hearing how your code works."

"It—it's kind of personal."

"If it's that personal, then we'd better take it down to the principal's office."

"No, I'll explain it. Here is the code message:

```
LYMEGI   SRTSNS   EPAXJN   EDTTTL
UAWYEE   LAHIEO   SOCDSH   EAARKY
```

What you do is make a big block of letters out of the message. The letters are written on blocked paper just the right size to match this grille."

"What is a grille?"

"It's this sort of mask, with some holes cut in it. You place it over the block of letters, and then you can read the message through the holes. It says: 'Miss Jewel is a—' and then you turn the grille around, top to bottom, to read the rest of the message. It says, well—"

"I can read it. 'Miss Jewel is a grand teacher.' What made you write a message like that?"

"I guess it was that time—" his voice quavered a little

9

"—that I threw the eraser and broke a window, and you *didn't* send a note home to my dad. Then I just knew that you had to be the very bestest—"

"Johnny, your grammar," Miss Jewel murmured. "If I am such a grand teacher, as you say, why was it necessary to write it in code?"

"Because I was only going to show it to a couple of friends of mine. I didn't want you to see it, or the rest of the class, because then they might think I was gunning for an A."

"Thank you, Johnny. I think you have just given me the most beautiful snow job I have ever seen. I wish I could give you an A in imagination, but unfortunately we don't grade in that subject."

Miss Jewel picked up the grille and placed it down again. Then she turned it around top to bottom. "Johnny," she said firmly, "I am now ordering you to stay after school for two hours every night for a week."

Johnny shuffled back to his seat, looking disappointed but not too surprised. Why was Miss Jewel so severe with poor Johnny?

ANSWER: Miss Jewel was clever enough to see that Johnny had used up only half the letters in the block, and that the other half contained another message. By turning the grille over to its reverse side, and then using it the same way Johnny had done, she was able to read the real message. Can you read it?

NOTE: This is a 48-position Cardan grille, based on the diagram on page 14. To make a similar grille, mark off a piece of cardboard into eight rows of six squares each. Number the squares according to the diagram and cut out 12 squares, making sure that each hole removes a different number. Most Cardan grilles are square, so that you can rotate the grille into four different positions without turning it over. Schemes for 25-, 36-, and 64-position square grilles are also given here.

L	Y	M	E	G	I
S	R	T	S	N	S
E	P	A	X	J	N
E	D	T	T	T	L
U	A	W	Y	E	E
L	A	H	I	E	O
S	O	C	D	S	H
E	A	A	R	K	Y

This is the block of letters which Johnny used to hide his code message. If you want to write another message, use another arrangement of letters.

The front side of the grille, which Johnny wanted Miss Jewel to see and use.

The reverse side of the grille, which Johnny did not want Miss Jewel to see.

```
 1  2  3  3  2  1
 4  5  6  6  5  4
 7  8  9  9  8  7
10 11 12 12 11 10
10 11 12 12 11 10
 7  8  9  9  8  7
 4  5  6  6  5  4
 1  2  3  3  2  1
```

48-position Cardan
grille

```
1 2 3 4 5 1
5 6 7 8 6 2
4 8 9 9 7 3
3 7 9 9 8 4
2 6 8 7 6 5
1 5 4 3 2 1
```

36-position Cardan
grille

```
1 2 3 4 1
4 5 6 5 2
3 6 X 6 3
2 5 6 5 4
1 4 3 2 1
```

25-position Cardan
grille

```
1  2  3  4  5  6  7  1
7  8  9 10 11 12  8  2
6 12 13 14 15 13  9  3
5 11 15 16 16 14 10  4
4 10 14 16 16 15 11  5
3  9 13 15 14 13 12  6
2  8 12 11 10  9  8  7
1  7  6  5  4  3  2  1
```

64-position Cardan
grille

MATCH OR MISMATCH?

To break the ice at a party, use Rogues' Gallery on page 18 to see if a couple is matched or mismatched. The boy will supposedly learn what the girl is really thinking about him.

Suppose that the boy was born April (the fourth month) 1st, 1955, and the girl was born September (the ninth month) 27th, 1957. Their key numbers are found by adding across the dates until only one digit is left:

```
BOY:   4 + 1 + 1 + 9 + 5 + 5 = 25 = 2 + 5 =        7
GIRL:  9 + 2 + 7 + 1 + 9 + 5 + 7 = 40 = 4 + 0 =    4
                                7 + 4 = 11 = 1 + 1 = 2
```

The total of their key numbers is 2, so look at No. 2 section on the Boy-Girl table. Because the boy's key number (7) is odd, he selects the odd message under "boy." The girl's number (4) is even, so she selects the even message under "girl." Copy one message right below the other:

O X Y G Q K Y U H M G D S H S F N

W U T S X Q K N G G S S E L Y T L

Now use Rogues' Gallery for combining every pair of letters. A ruler is very helpful for following the chart. Find O in the column at the side and W in the line across the top (or vice versa). Follow the lines across and down until they intersect (at T), the first letter. X and U intersect at H; Y and T intersect at I, and so on:

T H I S I S F U N . . .

The message may turn out to be enthusiastic, warm, cool— or a jumble (zero, nothing). But if you don't like your message, you can try it again—using phone numbers instead of birth dates!

BOY-GIRL TABLE

Boy

1. Odd	HUJJK	OEWUA	CUZBZ	RP
Even	XVXOE	OEBYG	KEOXR	RC
2. Odd	OXYGQ	KYUHM	GDSHS	FN
Even	MEFWQ	PBXHA	NZLVH	WJ
3. Odd	FFTGV	VPXHY	SUPTZ	IT
Even	RVGEB	WCXRD	ABTQN	MZ
4. Odd	YAVRR	VXQDI	AQJOK	NK
Even	DFEKO	SGPPI	CMAHV	PS
5. Odd	XYGVD	WHPSJ	GDOXW	AB
Even	WJANL	ZMJSE	LVXGQ	QK
6. Odd	WYZNA	UMCGM	IAEMK	DL
Even	AJOWJ	PMHGF	BCMKI	IN
7. Odd	FTSLV	RRZNA	TEXKM	QR
Even	FYTNM	GNVAG	FEAZU	SF
8. Odd	NAOQH	JSYLE	IFXNR	KY
Even	YCSPZ	HIHPI	XSLMY	IU
9. Odd	VZLFU	NUQTD	TKLUG	CR
Even	GCMML	MNVZY	KGTKV	HL

Girl

| 1. Odd | DVCQT | QMOVF | LQWUE | YO |
| Even | VZOXM | NTINT | CCOQT | AH |

| 2. Odd | WVNOK | HOFVQ | EBMGJ | SD |
| Even | WUTSX | QKNGG | SSELY | TL |

| 3. Odd | CMVRH | CGYTI | FVDEM | LC |
| Even | ERMSB | VKSND | CSFHV | GM |

| 4. Odd | ARHKI | ZPOLB | EMAPH | IW |
| Even | DGURW | HFEVR | WELXB | FA |

| 5. Odd | UZWOJ | HTSPQ | EGETX | PI |
| Even | SHXDJ | YQQYP | MMAAB | EK |

| 6. Odd | WHPYG | NBIFX | JHZFJ | JQ |
| Even | YOGOG | SLAMT | QKZRL | JY |

| 7. Odd | BWNLN | AIHLQ | DVYRF | GG |
| Even | LYXVK | AYHSA | RNBSE | GY |

| 8. Odd | DWFEQ | JYPSJ | CPNLN | CP |
| Even | WKZXG | YZOCL | GKULH | RI |

| 9. Odd | NWCTI | FDHIY | BOTPX | SN |
| Even | JKZCP | LNDIN | BOKOO | CN |

17

ROGUES' GALLERY

	A	B	C	D	E	F	G	H	I	J	K	L	M	N	O	P	Q	R	S	T	U	V	W	X	Y	Z
A	Q	D	S	B	U	N	O	R	J	I	P	M	L	F	G	K	A	H	C	X	E	Z	Y	T	W	V
B	D	M	G	A	K	H	C	F	O	X	E	Z	B	P	I	N	Y	W	V	U	T	S	R	J	Q	L
C	S	G	U	F	W	D	B	T	L	N	O	I	R	J	K	Q	P	M	A	H	C	X	E	V	Z	Y
D	B	A	F	H	J	C	X	D	I	E	Z	Y	N	M	P	O	W	V	U	T	S	R	Q	G	L	K
E	U	K	W	J	Z	G	F	V	R	D	B	N	T	L	Q	S	O	I	P	M	A	H	C	Y	X	E
F	N	H	D	C	G	X	E	B	P	Z	Y	W	O	A	M	I	V	U	T	S	R	Q	L	F	K	J
G	O	C	B	X	F	E	Z	N	M	Y	W	V	I	H	A	P	U	T	S	R	Q	L	K	D	J	G
H	R	F	T	D	V	B	N	S	K	O	I	P	Q	G	J	L	M	A	H	C	X	E	Z	U	Y	W
I	J	O	L	I	R	P	M	K	D	A	H	C	G	N	B	F	X	E	Z	Y	W	V	U	Q	T	S
J	I	X	N	E	D	Z	Y	O	A	W	V	U	P	C	H	M	T	S	R	Q	L	K	J	B	G	F
K	P	E	O	Z	B	Y	W	I	H	V	U	T	M	X	C	A	S	R	Q	L	K	J	G	N	F	D
L	M	Z	I	Y	N	W	V	P	C	U	T	S	A	E	X	H	R	Q	L	K	J	G	F	O	D	B
M	L	B	R	N	T	O	I	Q	G	P	M	A	K	D	F	J	H	C	X	E	Z	Y	W	S	V	U
N	F	P	J	M	L	A	H	G	N	C	X	E	D	I	O	B	Z	Y	W	V	U	T	S	K	R	Q
O	G	I	K	P	Q	M	A	J	B	H	C	X	F	O	N	D	E	Z	Y	W	V	U	T	L	S	R
P	K	N	Q	O	S	I	P	L	F	M	A	H	J	B	D	G	C	X	E	Z	Y	W	V	R	U	T
Q	A	Y	P	W	O	V	U	M	X	T	S	R	H	Z	E	C	Q	L	K	J	G	F	D	I	B	N
R	H	W	M	V	I	U	T	A	E	S	R	Q	C	Y	Z	X	L	K	J	G	F	D	B	P	N	O
S	C	V	A	U	P	T	S	H	Z	R	Q	L	X	W	Y	E	K	J	G	F	D	B	N	M	O	I
T	X	U	H	T	M	S	R	C	Y	Q	L	K	E	V	W	Z	J	G	F	D	B	N	O	A	I	P
U	E	T	C	S	A	R	Q	X	W	L	K	J	Z	U	V	Y	G	F	D	B	N	O	I	H	P	M
V	Z	S	X	R	H	Q	L	E	V	K	J	G	Y	T	U	W	F	D	B	N	O	I	P	C	M	A
W	Y	R	E	Q	C	L	K	Z	U	J	G	F	W	S	T	V	D	B	N	O	I	P	M	X	A	H
X	T	J	V	G	Y	F	D	U	Q	B	N	O	S	K	L	R	I	P	M	A	H	C	X	W	E	Z
Y	W	Q	Z	L	X	K	J	Y	T	G	F	D	V	R	S	U	B	N	O	I	P	M	A	E	H	C
Z	V	L	Y	K	E	J	G	W	S	F	D	B	U	Q	R	T	N	O	I	P	M	A	H	Z	C	X

NOTE: This is a reciprocal Vigenère table, nicknamed Rogues' Gallery. A Vigenère is used to change substitution alphabets a number of times within the same message. "Reciprocal" means that messages are read in exactly the same way they are written.

To use this table in the most common way, the parties agree on a secret key word in advance, such as WOLF. Start by writing the message down, and carefully copy a letter of the key word below each letter:

Message:	P R E P A R E T O L E A V E
Key:	W O L F W O L F W O L F W O

Now use the Rogues' Gallery table to combine letters. (Lay a ruler across the desired line, and read down the column with a pencil.) P and W, the first letter of the message and the first letter of the key, intersect at V. R and O, the second letters of the message and the key, combine into Z. And so on, until you have:

Cipher: V Z N I Y Z N S T X N N P Q

Want to know how the Rogues' Gallery table given here was made? It was based on the word EXCHAMPION, plus the remaining letters of the alphabet in order. The first few lines were written as follows:

	E	X	C	H	A	M	P	I	O	N	B	D	F	G	J	K	L	Q	R	S	T	U	V	W	Y	Z
E	Z	Y	W	V	U	T	S	R	Q	L	K	J	G	F	D	B	N	O	I	P	M	A	H	C	X	E
X	Y	W	V	U	T	S	R	Q	L	K	J	G	F	D	B	N	O	I	P	M	A	H	C	X	E	Z
C	W	V	U	T	S	R	Q	L	K	J	G	F	D	B	N	O	I	P	M	A	H	C	X	E	Z	Y

Notice that the second line is simply the top line in reverse, but with each following line moved one position to the left.

When complete, this table will give exactly the same results as the full reciprocal Vigenère table given on page 18. However, so it can be used most conveniently, cut the columns into long strips and correctly arrange them, so that the indicator line across the top (EXCHA . . .) is a normal alphabet. Then the same thing can be done with the horizontal lines.

A PRIVATE DIARY

A diary is a record of growth. You can use it just to record the events of each day, for everyone to read, but an engagement book or calendar would serve that purpose equally well. Your private diary will show what made each day different for you and memorable compared to all others—such as an unexpected happening, your new insight, your reaction to external events, something beautiful that you witnessed or thought of, your triumphs and consolations. This diary can be a fascinating, private document to come back to in later years.

Your private battles should, to some extent, be fought out in private. Is anyone entitled to know your innermost thoughts? No, not your parents, or your husband or wife, or your government. Why not, if you aren't doing anything to be ashamed of? Because many thoughts are transient, a groping for truth, and are often never meant to be acted upon. Moreover, a person who tells everything about himself soon becomes a terrible bore. We naturally select what we tell, and our choice depends in part upon who our listener is.

In an increasingly crowded world, with snoopers and eaves-dropping devices everywhere and computers assembling all this data into mammoth files, our privacy is more precious than ever, something to be cherished and to struggle for. If codes can be a small aid in protecting our privacy, they are a valuable tool.

Anti-Snoopers

If you intend to put your diary into code, how difficult a system do you want? Part of the problem is the amount of work involved, and part concerns the ease of rereading—what is called retrieving information. If you intend to put your diary away and not come back to it for many years, you can use a difficult system—hopefully, you will not have lost the keys or tables by the time you need them. But if you cannot safeguard your diary itself, how can you safeguard your code?

There are many simple codes which are not very safe. But they are easy to use. They may scare away a person who thinks a diary or notebook or letter not under lock and key is public property. The code may tingle his conscience, or it may make him decide that reading your diary isn't worth the trouble, or it may scare him by warning that he might get caught!

If you have any special knowledge of shorthand or a foreign language, that might be sufficient to safeguard your diary. Special friends can be designated by special code words. Simply reversing the letters in every word often proves effective. Reversing the order of the words sometimes does it too. Running all the letters together and breaking them into groups of five or at random works also. Here is a way of breaking words apart by dropping the letter E:

PR PAR TOL AV TU SDAY V NING

Combinations of these ideas are more effective.

Lincoln's Rail Fence

For this code, print the letters neatly in blocks, as if on graph paper. A message could be divided into two lines and written as follows:

```
I   A   A   O   D   R   U   T   M
  H   D   W   N   E   F   L   I   E
```

Then other letters can fill in the blank spaces:

```
I AATAI OHDARTURTAMC
L HSDNWGNTEFFELDI NE
```

These latter letters might continue the message, be nulls (letters without meaning), or a second message with a different cipher.

Another system of Rail Fence would be written like this:

```
I    H    A    D    A    W    O
  N    D    E    R    F    U    L
    T    I    M    E    L    A    S
      T    N    I    G    H    T    A
        F    T    E    R    D    A    N
```

Then assemble all the letters:

INTTF HDINT AEMIE DREGR AFLHD WUATA OLSAN

For an alternate method, write the correct message in diagonal lines; then assemble the letters reading across the lines.

Zombie

This system uses a scrambled alphabet which is written out on a tape and placed above the top line when a message is being written or read:

```
V H I J C K T L O MR N Y P A Q B S D U E WF X G Z

N   A           I   H   D   A   W   O
```

The example shows how the letters I HAD A WON would be entered. The first letter is written under A, the second letter under B, the third letter under C, and so on.

Though this is the common Zombie, an alternate way, though not so safe, is more convenient to use. Start writing the message vertically below A, for as many lines as you care to go, then continue under B, and so on:

```
V H I J C K T L O MR N Y P A Q B S D U E WF X G Z
        R               I   W
        F               H   O
        U               A   N
        L               D   D
        T               A   E
```

Then, when you are finished, hide your tape!

THE PROWLER IN THE TYPING CLASS

The school was very upset. Just last week an unidentified caller said that a bomb was about to go off, so the school had been emptied and searched. Nothing was found and no bomb went off. It was just a hoax, but everyone was still nervous.

"Why would anyone plant a bomb, and then call up to warn people?" wondered Miss Young, the typing teacher.

"You don't know what kind of warped mind you are dealing with," Miss Grayson warned her. "There is a certain kind of person who wants to make a nuisance of himself to feel important, but doesn't really want to hurt anyone."

Nevertheless, Miss Grayson remained alert. One morning while classes were passing, she noticed a boy with a package under his arm look around carefully and then slip into Miss Young's classroom. Miss Grayson hurried up the corridor as fast as she could through the crowd of students. The door to the typing room was open and she went inside. No one was there, but the room had a rear door and the boy must have slipped out that door just as Miss Grayson came in the front.

Miss Grayson quickly looked around the room. She did not find a bomb, but she did find something. At this moment, Miss Young came into the room with Mr. Breen, the assistant principal. Miss Grayson explained about the suspected bomb.

"That boy looked as guilty as Cain," she concluded.

"Maybe because he knew he didn't belong in here," said Miss Young, smiling. "The next class is all girls."

"It shouldn't take long to search the room," Mr. Breen suggested.

"I searched it already. And I found—*this*." Miss Grayson pointed dramatically to a sheet of typing paper in a typewriter at the rear of the room. Miss Young rolled the paper out of the machine. It read:

Upit ;imvj od pm yp½ djr;g pg vsnomry/

"Why would a bomber leave a code message like this?"

"Because there was someone in the class he knew, someone he wanted to warn. Who sits at this desk?" Miss Grayson asked.

"No one this period," Miss Young replied. "It's an extra desk."

"And he knew it. We don't have very much time. The bomb may go off any minute." Miss Grayson looked worried.

"But you didn't find any bomb," Mr. Breen pointed out.

"Not in *this* room. He may have taken it out again and planted it somewhere else. He certainly didn't have very long to write that message. I was here in a minute."

"Are you sure it's from this typewriter?" asked Mr. Breen.

"Oh, yes," Miss Young answered. "The type matches this typewriter perfectly."

Miss Grayson looked at her watch, as though she were ticking off the seconds. Suddenly Miss Young smiled. "I know how to read this. It will only take half a minute."

Can you figure out how to read the message? If you do not know how to touch type, ask a typist to help you.

ANSWER: "This boy wanted to write a message very quickly," Miss Young pointed out. "Possibly the person he wanted to meet wasn't here yet, and he couldn't wait. So he put his paper in the machine and moved his fingers one position to the *right* of the normal position, and typed his message. I can read it by putting my fingers one position to the *left* of the normal position and typing the message he left in the machine."

She typed quickly, and the answer came out:

Your lunch is on top shelf of cabinet.

"I've had lots of experience with fingers on wrong keys," she explained. "You know, he may not have even intended it to be a code message. He was in a hurry, and put his fingers on the wrong keys by accident."

WHEEL OF FORTUNE

You can use the large grille here and the matching block or tableau of letters to tell fortunes. If the player was born during daylight (6:00 A.M. to 6:00 P.M.), use the front side of the grille; if he was born in nighttime, use the reverse side. Turn the grille so that the season in which he was born (according to the calendar) is across the top; then lay the grille on the block of letters and read the letters which show through.

To make the grille, take a piece of cardboard and cut out 21 holes, each one through a different number, as in the

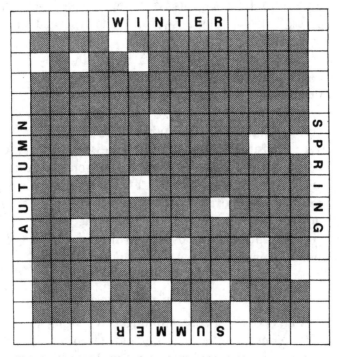

This is the right side of the grille. Use it if you were born during the daytime.

number chart on page 29. If the grille is going to be turned over, do not cut any holes in the main diagonals, where the X's are in the chart.

You can use other size grilles also. Another variation is to use two grilles over the same block of letters; the first grille picks up some of the letters, and the other grille the remainder.

Now wouldn't you know that a wheel of fortune would be square?

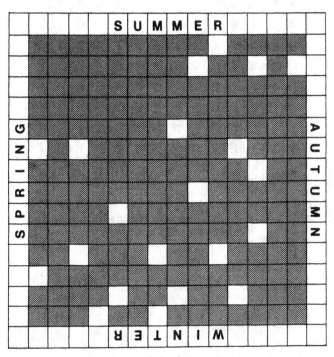

Use the reverse side of the grille, shown here, if you were born during the nighttime.

Q	A	T	F	B	Y	O	C	H	M	H	O	T	X
R	F	O	I	R	K	L	W	U	L	H	S	F	T
A	C	O	I	A	U	T	K	R	N	S	O	E	I
D	C	T	R	T	O	W	C	A	E	R	H	W	H
T	T	I	U	T	R	E	O	O	T	O	R	U	T
B	A	E	N	E	U	I	V	U	L	Y	H	O	E
Y	N	A	W	O	L	N	N	Y	E	L	A	I	D
A	I	I	S	A	R	E	E	L	L	D	O	I	D
U	M	W	T	L	W	L	F	W	T	A	C	B	H
O	Y	S	E	H	D	I	I	I	H	R	O	S	S
O	U	F	E	O	T	T	O	C	H	E	N	H	A
E	E	E	E	C	S	T	E	S	O	T	E	S	M
L	L	L	E	R	I	N	U	T	D	L	I	L	N
Y	P	I	E	T	E	S	E	T	G	D	R	S	Z

To tell your fortune, place one of the grilles from pages 26-27 on this block of letters. The words which are spelled out may tell you things you did not know!

```
X  1  2  3  4  5  6  6  5  4  3  2  1 X
1  X  7  8  9 10 11 11 10  9  8  7  X 1
2  7  X 12 13 14 15 15 14 13 12  X  7 2
3  8 12  X 16 17 18 18 17 16  X 12  8 3
4  9 13 16  X 19 20 20 19  X 16 13  9 4
5 10 14 17 19  X 21 21  X 19 17 14 10 5
6 11 15 18 20 21  X  X 21 20 18 15 11 6
6 11 15 18 20 21  X  X 21 20 18 15 11 6
5 10 14 17 19  X 21 21  X 19 17 14 10 5
4  9 13 16  X 19 20 20 19  X 16 13  9 4
3  8 12  X 16 17 18 18 17 16  X 12  8 3
2  7  X 12 13 14 15 15 14 13 12  X  7 2
1  X  7  8  9 10 11 11 10  9  8  7  X 1
X  1  2  3  4  5  6  6  5  4  3  2  1 X
```

To determine which squares to cut out on your grille, refer to this chart of numbers. Cut 21 squares in the grille, each one through a different number. Do not cut out any squares marked "X."

```
            1   2   3   3   2   1
            4   5   6   6   5   4
            7   8   9   9   8   7
1  4  7  X  10  11  11  10  X  7  4  1
2  5  8 10  X  12  12  X  10  8  5  2
3  6  9 11  12  X   X  12  11  9  6  3
3  6  9 11  12  X   X  12  11  9  6  3
2  5  8 10  X  12  12  X  10  8  5  2
1  4  7  X  10  11  11  10  X  7  4  1
            7   8   9   9   8   7
            4   5   6   6   5   4
            1   2   3   3   2   1
```

Sometimes wheels of fortune are other shapes too. Here are diagrams for rotating, reversible grilles in the shape of a cross and an irregular octagon. Do not use those positions with an X.

```
              1   2   2   1
          3   4   5   5   4   3
      X   6   7   8   8   7   6   X
   3  6  X   9  10  10   9   X   6   3
1  4  7  9   X  11  11   X   9   7   4   1
2  5  8 10  11   X   X  11  10   8   5   2
2  5  8 10  11   X   X  11  10   8   5   2
1  4  7  9   X  11  11   X   9   7   4   1
   3  6  X   9  10  10   9   X   6   3
      X   6   7   8   8   7   6   X
          3   4   5   5   4   3
              1   2   2   1
```

THE RABBIT FARM

Aaron was paying his first visit to Warren O'Hare's Rabbit Farm. It was a new business and didn't seem to be going very well.

"No, I haven't sold any rabbits yet," Mr. O'Hare admitted. "And of course they really aren't rabbits anyway. American rabbits are too wild to make good pets. These are European hares."

Aaron thought the animals, though cute, were pretty much alike.

"They all came from one pair," Mr. O'Hare explained. "When I got up to a hundred, I decided to go into business. Sure you wouldn't like to pick out a couple? I don't sell them to just anybody. If I don't think they would take proper care of them, I refuse to sell."

"I should think a lot of kids would like to buy rabbits," Aaron observed.

"Oh, they would. But the parents always say no."

Aaron noticed that there was a row of cages outside the shed. Each cage held one rabbit, and on each cage was a number. They read:

24 43 04 15 12 73 21 10 19 16 13 26 31 54 30 02 33 08 40 14 77 71 53 42 09 63 41 50 82 38

"What do the numbers mean?" Aaron asked.

"Well, at first I tried to give the rabbits names, but when I got too many I gave them numbers instead."

"Is there any reason why the cages are in that order?"

"That's my secret," said Mr. O'Hare, with a tiny smile.

"Well, are the cages always in that order?"

"No, sometimes I place them in a different order. It's a whim of mine."

To Aaron it looked as though the numbers could be some kind of code, but he didn't see how that were possible, since there were more than 26 cages, and no number was repeated.

He explained that he hadn't come to buy, but was just looking. Mr. O'Hare seemed disappointed, but put a business card into his hand anyway, just in case he should change his mind.

"Maybe I could teach them tricks and charge admission," the owner mused.

Aaron looked at the business card. On one side it was just an ordinary card, but on the other side was the following table:

```
J Y A H T E I C L P
U D G WK S N B X R
E L E C K G S U N A
H WO R B I R D A E
P I E T F V E N S Y
R L T T E C Q H A G
MZ O MH E O D F U
T O A L WT F S D T
A N E A I O O E N R
Z K X N Q V J M I E
```

Aaron wondered if this had anything to do with the way the cages were arranged, and if the numbers were a code, how he could read the message. He realized, of course, that the deciphered message was just an advertising gimmick rather than any great secret. Can you read it?

ANSWER: Place the digits from 1 through 0 across the top, and again in a column down the left side. Then you can easily read the message. The first number of Mr. O'Hare's cages is 24. Find 2 in the left column, and read over to the column headed 4, and the first letter is W; 43 will give the letter 0, and so on.

The same table can be written in a different form, which makes it a little easier to write messages:

$$
\begin{array}{llllllll}
A & 13 & 30 & 49 & 69 & 83 & 91 & 94 \\
B & 28 & 45 \\
C & 18 & 34 & 66 & . & . & .
\end{array}
$$

There are other forms of Rabbit Farm. The following table can also be used:

	1	2	3	4	5	6	7	8	9	0
1, 4, 7	V	I	C	T	O	R	Y	A	B	D
2, 5, 8	E	F	G	H	J	K	L	M	N	P
3, 6, 9	Q	S	U	W	X	Z				

V could be written as either 11, 41, or 71. K could be written as 26, 56, or 86. A message might read:

$$
\begin{array}{ccccccccccc}
A & L & L & Q & U & I & E & T & H & E & R & E \\
18 & 87 & 57 & 31 & 63 & 42 & 51 & 14 & 84 & 51 & 76 & 21
\end{array}
$$

This table may also be written long vertically instead of long horizontally.

Another possible table is a square five letters across by five down, omitting letter Z:

	1–6	2–7	3–8	4–9	5–0
1–6	V	I	C	T	O
2–7	R	Y	A	B	D
3–8	E	F	G	H	J
4–9	K	L	M	N	P
5–0	Q	S	U	W	X

V could be written as 11, 16, 61, or 66. M could be written as 43, 48, 93, or 98. A message might read:

$$
\begin{array}{ccccccccccc}
A & L & L & Q & U & I & E & T & H & E & R & E \\
23 & 97 & 47 & 51 & 58 & 17 & 36 & 14 & 84 & 36 & 76 & 31
\end{array}
$$

Rabbit Farm II

Any message given under Rabbit Farm can be made more difficult by changing the coded message in numbers to letters with the following table:

1	2	3	4	5	6	7	8	9	0
V	I	C	T	O	R	Y	A	B	D
E	F	G	H	J	K	L	M	N	P
Q	S	U	W	X	Z	&	.	?	/

For example, 3 may be changed into either C, G, or U. The message just given could be written as the bottom line here:

A	L	L	Q	U	I	E	T	H	E	R	E
23	97	47	51	58	17	36	14	84	36	76	31
SC	B&	TL	OV	O.	QY	CR	VW	MH	CR	YZ	UV

GREMLIN CORRESPONDENCE

Pen pals may want to conduct part of their correspondence in code, for secrecy or just for fun. The Gremlin (better known as Gronsfeld) is well suited for that purpose. To write the message "Dick lost our ship's rudder at Carlton," use the key number 56928. Copy down the message and write the key number continuously below the letters:

```
D I C K L O S T O U R S H I  P S R U D D E R A T C A R L T O N
5 6 9 2 8 5 6 9 2 8 5 6 9 2 8 5 6 9 2 8 5 6 9 2 8 5 6 9 2 8 5
```

Write the coded message by using the letter in the alphabet which is the required number of spaces further down the alphabet. The fifth letter after D is I, so that becomes the first cipher letter. The sixth letter after I is O. The ninth letter after C is L. The message would be written:

```
I O L M T T Y C Q C W Y Q K X X X D F L J X J V K F X U V WS
```

If you find it easier to remember key words rather than key numbers, use the following table:

1	2	3	4	5	6	7	8	9
A	B	C	D	E	F	G	H	I
J	K	L	M	N	O	P	Q	R
S	T	U	V	W	X	Y	Z	

With this easy-to-remember table, the key word NORTH gives the key number 56928.

More advanced Gremlinites may be able to read a coded message without knowing the key number. To do this, copy the alphabet in reverse below each letter of the message that was received, through nine lines:

```
I  O L MT T Y C Q C WY Q K X X X D F L J X J V K F X U V WS
H N K L S S X B P B V X P J WWWC E K I  WI  U J E WT U V R
G MJ  K R R WA O A U WO I  V V V B D J H V H T I  D V S T U Q
F L I  J Q Q V Z N Z T V N H U U U A C I  G U G S H C U R S T P
E K H I  P P U Y MY S U MG T T T Z B H F T F R G B T Q R S O
D J G H O O T X L X R T L F S S S Y A G E S E Q F A S P Q R N
C I  F G N N S WK WQ S K E R R R X Z F D R D P E Z R O P Q M
B H E F MMR V J V P R J D Q Q Q WY E C Q C O D Y Q N O P L
A G D E L L Q U I  U O Q I  C P P P V X D B P B N C X P MN O K
Z F C D K K P T H T N P H B O O O U WC A O A MB WO L MN J
```

If you know that the key number consists of five digits, you can experiment to find exactly what it is. Choose any letter in the first column, then the letter five positions to the right on the same horizontal line, and five positions after that, until you discover which line is the most likely. Then you do the same for the second letter: Choose any letter in the second column and find what letters come after it in the same horizontal row at intervals of five letters. Sooner or later you will find the right combination of letters.

If you do not know how many digits are in the key number, your task is more difficult. You can, of course, simply test for key numbers of various lengths. If you discover the rhythm of the message, however, you have found a short cut: certain letters and combinations of letters in a message may appear at certain intervals, such as five or multiples of five.

Another approach, if you do not know the number of digits in the key number, is to choose any first and second letters from the first two columns. Eventually you will try D and I. Move one row to the right and see what other combinations you get, using the position of D and I. You find JF (bad), GG (not good), HN (unlikely), ON (a logical combination of letters suggesting a key number of four digits; later, though, you get SX, which is bad), and OS (possible, and as it turns out, correct). Knowing the first two letters of every five, you should have little trouble with the remainder.

To defeat the more advanced Gremlin decoder, a message need not be written using the regular alphabet. Use a scrambled alphabet instead:

V I C T O R Y A B D E F G H J K L M N P Q S U W X Z

Using this table, the same message with the same key number would be written:

```
D I C K L O S T O U R . . .
5 6 9 2 8 5 6 9 2 8 5 . . .
J A F M X D I G Y O E . . .
```

```
F    F    F   BOARD
A    O    U
M    R    T
E    T    U
     U    R
     N    E
     E
```

Use the table here to tell your fortune by spelling out meaning-ful words. Place a button or marker on the center E. Throw a pair of dice. If the numbers that appear are five and two, for example, you may move seven letters in any direction—up or down, right or left (not diagonal); or you may move five letters in one direction and two in another, including backwards; or you may move two spaces in one direction and five in another. Only the final letter that you land on counts.

You must be very quiet and seek the guidance of the mystic spirit to tell you in what direction to take your moves. Write down each letter you finally land on for that turn. At first you will probably accumulate a meaningless string of letters, but sooner or later a word or phrase will be spelled out. Regard messages of three letters as coincidence; four-letter messages are doubtful; but messages of five or more letters are probably important. Think hard about the meaning of this message.

If you have more than one player, each may take a turn. When a player's turn comes around again, he should move from the point where he left off last, *unless the minute hand on the clock has passed 12.* In this case he must start from the center again. No player's turn may run past the 12 on the clock, or the mystic spirit will be offended. If a player loses his place and is not sure where he belongs, he must rely on the mystic spirit to guide him correctly.

P.S. If you don't believe in mystic spirits, have fun anyway.

F F F BOARD

```
E S F L Y A N E R W O T K H I D E B G R A O N H T
T N A R C S E H G A E M T I O D B E S F L Y A N E
U H C L I T M O W N A S E R I N Z P T F E D O E S
L E L E H V S T A N C O D Y E R U I F O Q H L R A
O S G B E S F L Y A N E R W O T K H I D E A U W P
D X N D N R E I D X S E H C L I T M O W B U T O T
E D A O J E R W O T K H I D E B G R A N G T N T I
F I M I T N F O Q H A U T J N R E I O A R J A K W
T E O T U A I T N A R C S E H G A D N S A N R H E
P R R M A Y U U G E X L M O D A E X H E O R C I R
Z N E E H L R L A I D H E T U K M S T R N E S D O
N J W A Q F E O E Z I G F Y A M T E E I H I E E M
I T I G O S Y D O B A W E C P N I H S N T D H B A
R U T H F E D E R Y S I L Q B U O C A Z E X G G N
E A P E I B O F A F N Q R W O I D L P P S S A R G
S H A S U D C T P V C J U K V S B I T T A E E A L
A Q S C R O N P I O X U T E H O J T I F P H M O E
N O E R E I A Z N I R E S A N W O M W E T C T N H
W F T A Y T T S V H E L G N A M O R E D I L I H V
O I H N D M E A G H E S C R A N T U L O W I O T S
M U N T O C N A T S V H E L G N A M O R E T D E T
T R O U L O D E F T P Z N I R E S A N W O M B S A
I E A R G B E D I H K T O W R E N A Y L F S E A N
L Y D O C N A T S V H E L G N A M O R E W I T P C
C H E S X D I E R N J T U A H Q O F I U R E Y D O
```

SPELLING HIVE

Besides telling fortunes, the FFF Board on page 39 may also be used for a game, when the mystic spirit is not present.

Use only one die. Place a marker or button on the center E, and take the number of spaces shown on the die in any direction (including diagonal). You must travel in the same direction for each roll of the die. Only the letter you finally land on counts. Write this letter down and throw the die again. If you land exactly on the border—one space beyond the letters—you may add any vowel you please, including Y, to your letters. After throwing the die again, you may re-enter the board from any letter on the outside that you choose.

The purpose of the game is to make as many words as possible containing four or more letters. When you complete a word, continue from the point where your marker stands and try to make another word. Continue until you fail to make a recognizable word, and then your turn is over. Here is how a typical turn may go:

```
T E A|S E
L E A|N S
WI S|E L Y
P I R . . . .
```

You began by rolling 4 and moved down from the center square to T. Then you shot 1, and moved one space to the right; shot another 1, and moved one space down; shot still another 1, and moved one space to the left; shot a 3, and moved three spaces down. You now have the word TEASE. Your next shot was 1, and you might have moved up and to the left for S, to make TEASES; but you overlooked it and moved one space to the right to L. Then you shot a 2, and moved down and to the right to E; shot a 1 and moved down to A; shot a 1 and moved to the left to N; shot a 2 and moved up and to the right to S—making LEANS. You shot a 3 and moved to the right to W; shot a 2 and moved northeast to I; shot a 3 and moved down to S; shot a 1 and moved to the right to E.

You next took a gamble. You had the word WISE, but having shot a 3, you moved left to L, and added the L to make WISEL. You were gambling that you would be able to reach Y on your next turn, to make WISELY. If you did not, you would lose the word WISE and your turn would be over. But you shot a 6 and moved northeast into the border, giving you the privilege of choosing Y. You then shot a 2, and chose to re-enter the board from the lower right corner, landing on P. You shot a 2, and moved to the left to I; shot a 1, and moved southwest to R; then shot a 2, and could find no letter useful to you, so you gave up your turn.

To compute your score, draw a vertical line after the third letters in the words, and count all the letters to the right of the line. In this turn, you scored seven. The next player begins his turn from the center E. The first player with 50 points wins.

CHALLENGE: Make up variations of this game:

1. Play with two dice, with no diagonal moves or "free" vowels when going into the border. You may "bend" your move as in fortune-telling, by travelling the number in one direction that appears on one die, and the rest of the spaces in another direction.

2. Each player has a marker and takes one throw at a time. Write down your letters in a string, and later put parentheses around the longest words you can make in your string.

3. The player wins who first spells out the name of a place (or athlete, or chemical element, or whatever).

4. A player can gain a special bonus if he announces in advance the word he is going to spell and makes it; but his turn ends if he fails to make it.

BIRTHDAY PROPHESIES

Here is a birthday message for you, though it might not be your birthday:

Q C N M D W E S U R X H J

To read it, use the Vigenère table on page 43. This contains 31 lines to allow for every day in a month. Take the date in the month on which you were born (the 6th, for instance) and lay a ruler just below that line on the table. Find each letter of the message in the alphabet across the top, and read down the column to the letter just above the ruler.

Using the 6th as your birth date, you would find Q in the top row above the line and trace down to line 6, to find B as the first true letter. Doing the same thing with C, the second code letter, you would find U, etc.

The message may not be clear and may need some thought. If it does not seem to apply to you right now, be careful; it may apply at any time up until a year after your next birthday. If you are curious, you can find out the code message for any of your friends by tracing out their birth dates.

If you are a skeptic, you may wonder how the same message could apply to all people born on the same day of the month. Here is the secret: Every person has his own personality, and interprets the message in the light of his own knowledge and ambitions. Thus, the same message has a different meaning for different people.

<u>A B C D E F G H I J K L M N O P Q R S T U V W X Y Z</u>

1. V J I W O X P A Q Y C U D N M L F T B K E S H R Z G
2. V D U R E X M G K S Y Z B T C L O A F J P H I N W Q
3. G P R E A K X T J H Q N V I L Z D O Y M S C W U B F
4. G O I S R B H K T Y F Z D N Q X W U E V L J A C P M
5. I B A M S G X C W K F J E V Y R H L T Z P D O U Q N
6. F X U D H G C E M R J K L I S Z B O Y A P N T W V Q
7. I H E W O B Y C U K M V T F J S L P N D G Q R A X Z
8. Q D I U A X W E L R M Z K C G B P T N F O Y S H V J
9. P B I Y U Z F H Q E G V D N S J M A R X L K O T C W
10. P H E U D L J K T S Y X O F V G W I B A R M N C Z Q
11. X J E M Q W H L Z Y N G A V F O R C U D I B P K T S
12. K L A P N C X I S M Q V O Y R H W T B F U Z E D J G
13. Z B A H O Q M K T Y S E G U C V L I R D P X F N J W
14. B Z L U N Y Q C F K H S G A D X P R O V T J E I W M
15. O Y P K H Z V L J D N X R A W B S U E M G Q T I C F
16. I Z A L N D X S M T V Y K C J F B U G W Q H O E R P
17. U Q R C O T D G L S Z X A E M Y P I F B W V H N K J
18. Z G O P C X M N B E D W R U K V Y F T Q S J A I H L
19. F X O Y A W B L K T Z J E N P V M U S X G C H I D R
20. I B A H S V Q E X Y J G C T R F W N D P O Z U K L M
21. B Y I W A F P E Q R M X G N Z U S O T K L J H V D C
22. M B I O T U Q A V Y J R K C W D S P H Z E X F L G N
23. H I E W Y R C N K G D V T S X Q B L U F P Z A O J M
24. K U Y R B I Q G X S V W A P D Z M O E F L H T N J C
25. H S X A N D G R C Y V F L P Z Q E J T W O K I U B M
26. J M A T F U Y E B R Z X K L S C W D I Q N G O H P V
27. F D E Y W Z J I X R U Q M G V S B H N L C P O A K T
28. W C H P N Y J R F A X M T O D U S E K G Z Q I B L V
29. S X N E F H P U Z B T R V A I G K C M J Y W O L D Q
30. G W L K R M Z E U D J X N I Q V S O Y A T H C B P F
31. Y L U F O C Z K T E B Q G N D X H P M J A V R I W S

MRS. STORMFIELD'S PECULIARITY

Susan thought she would like her new job as a salesclerk. Her supervisor, Mrs. Stormfield, was very helpful in showing her around the department and in explaining how the prices were marked. Susan noticed some queer markings on the merchandise and asked about them:

INC   MR   IPRA   IOE   TOP

Mrs. Stormfield explained that this was a code telling how much the store had paid for the item. Of course the store didn't want the customers to know the cost, because they might think that the price they had to pay was too high and that the store was making too much profit.

Susan wondered if she would ever be able to read this cost code. Then she realized that Mrs. Stormfield was making a strange speech, so she listened closely:

"You have done stenograph work, have studied mineralogy, and danced with a tambourine. We expect you to be methodical and to take the precaution of checking each subtrahend before you put the sales slip into the duplicator, or else the firm may face bankruptcy. This is not a playground, and I promulgate the regulation that you be productive. No doubt you would rather be a playwright with a manuscript on polytheism, but your wishes must be sublimated.

"You will meet many kinds of people, some who have just come from the motherland, some who are Republican, some phlegmatic, some prudential, and some who have the misfortune to have been recently inoculated. It is of the most *importance* that you be hospitable and sympathize with them. The work is exhausting, and you may develop wanderlust and wish to stroll on the boulevards in a mackintosh, but I have championed you and hope that I may rhapsodize over your work."

Needless to say, Susan found this speech very bewildering, but she remembered some of it and later wrote it down. If you were Susan, could you have figured out exactly what was peculiar about the way Mrs. Stormfield talked?

Then, could you have figured out how to read the code that Susan had noticed before?

ANSWER: Of course it is obvious that Mrs. Stormfield was using many big words. But did you notice that each big word she used had ten letters, and that the ten letters were never repeated in any one word? Such words (or sometimes two shorter words put together) are useful for cost codes, like this:

1 2 3 4 5 6 7 8 9 0
I M P O R T A N C E

Because Mrs. Stormfield stressed this word, and because these letters were used in the coded markings Susan had noticed, this must be the code word. The prices were:

$1.89   25¢ $13.57 $1.40 $6.43

If Susan had known from the beginning that the cost code was based on a word, she could have played around with the 10 different letters of the code until she made the word "importance." But Mrs. Stormfield's speech, confusing as it was, gave her an additional hint.

SURREPTITIOUS WRITING

There are normal and sound reasons why a person might want to conceal a secret message in a letter which seems quite open. College students, writing home, may be able to confide only in one parent because the other worries too much. There may be a message of affection for a special person. Business associates sometimes have a personal relationship, but they know that their letters will go through someone in the office before reaching the proper desk.

There are many ways you can disguise messages. The line of a graph may reach up to certain points (of sales, supposedly), but actually represent letters of the alphabet. A musical staff could hide a message, except from a trained musician. A grocery list could convey a secret meaning by the items ordered or their arrangement. A math problem could hide figures which are used as a key number in an already-established code. Playing cards could be assembled in a pre-arranged order, a message written on the edge, and then shuffled. Window shades, clothes on a line, or articles in a display window could be arranged to convey a message.

Gloria Scott

Gloria Scott systems, named after a Sherlock Holmes story, depend upon picking up words or letters at certain intervals. One method is to place a grille over a blank sheet and write the message through the holes of the grille. Then remove the grille and write a covering message over the whole page.

You might read the fifth word and every fifth word thereafter:

> If you decide to delay your coming ocean trip, will your country estate then be listed for possible sale very soon? It would be unwise to sell now.

or the first letter in every word:

> We have ever remained enthusiastic about Roy's electric trombone he energetically blows. Oh, our kids sing along. Nuts! Did Roy ever comment on Russ Dean's saying you overlooked us; perhaps, Russ observed, Mary is so extra determined—do and die. Delighted about Vera Ingram's dance.

or the second letter in every word:

> Any posters should not appear here.

Bacon's Alphabet

It is possible to write a message using only two different symbols, a system used in many computers. Morse code is another example, though of course it is not secret. As letters are not represented by an equal number of symbols, there must be a break after each letter. Francis Bacon's alphabet (slightly revised here to fit a modern alphabet) does use an equal number of symbols for each letter:

A	11111	H	11222	O	12221	V	21212
B	11112	I	12111	P	12222	W	21221
C	11121	J	12112	Q	21111	X	21222
D	11122	K	12121	R	21112	Y	22111
E	11211	L	12122	S	21121	Z	22112
F	11212	M	12211	T	21122		
G	11221	N	12212	U	21211		

Here is how a short message might be written, using the table as Bacon intended:

```
     H           A           L           T
1 1 2 2 2/1 1 1 1 1/1 2 1 2 2/2 1 1 2 2
F O u r s C O R E A N d S e v e N Y e a
```

You can write any message at all on the bottom line. The

important point is that a capital letter stands for digit 1, and a small or lower case letter stands for digit 2.

Of course this method is too obvious, and Bacon intended to be a little more secret. If the differences between the two kinds of letters were very slight, possibly roman and italic type, or bold face and regular, or two different styles of type, it might go unnoticed. The possibility of such slight differences has led to the legend that Francis Bacon is the real author of Shakespeare's plays, and there is a code message concealed in them somewhere that proves it!

You can use Bacon's alphabet in many ways besides letters, too. Here is a method of using it in blocks: an empty box stands for digit 1, and a box with an X stands for digit 2:

H			X	X	X
A					
L		X		X	X
T	X			X	X

This is simple to use if graph paper is available and space is not restricted. You might disguise this by labelling it an attendance report or some other kind of record.

Siesta

There is a hidden meaning in this message:

Aunt Adelaide is going to have two garden suppers annually.

Read it with the following table:

1	2	3	4	5	6	7	8	9	0
T	A	H	S	W	I	O	B	F	C
Y	U	E	G	R	L	D	N	P	M
V	J	K	Q	Z	X				

Take the first letter of each word in the message, and find the proper digit on the table:

A A I G T H T G S A
2 2 6 4 1 3 1 4 4 2

The message is 226–41 314–42. In a certain dictionary which both you and your friend have, you could look on page 226, word 41, and find "mission"; and look on page 314, word 42, for "successful."

Siesta is useful for hiding numerical information in an alphabetical cipher message.

River Styx

A	22	F	32	K	42	P	52	U	62
B	23	G	33	L	43	Q	53	V	63
C	24	H	34	M	44	R	54	W	64
D	25	I	35	N	45	S	55	X	65
E	26	J	36	O	46	T	56	Y	66

To write the message, "Leave today," first copy the appropriate number below each letter of the message:

L   E   A   V   E   T   O   D   A   Y
43 26 22 63 26 56 46 25 22 66

Our task now is to write a covering message in which each word will carry the correct number of letters. The first word should have four letters; the second word three letters; the third word (one or) two letters; the fourth word six (or more) letters. The message could be written:

When one is eating, he is likely not to notice which courses were burned, if there is an argument progressing.

Alphabet tables can also use punctuation marks or other symbols.

THE CLOCK GRILLE

This grille will give a one-word message which describes the essence of your character.

Find out the exact hour of your birth. Disregard the minutes; even if you were born at 3:59, your hour is still 3. Lay the grille

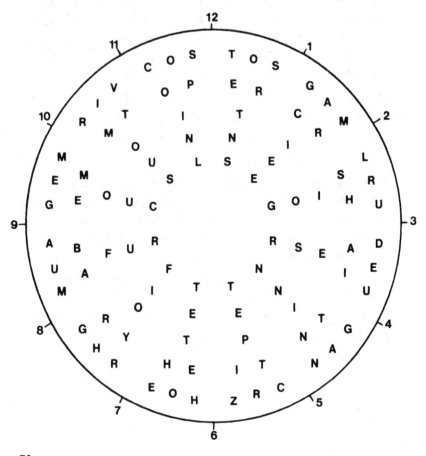

on the circle of letters with the arrow pointing to your hour. Read the message clockwise around the circle.

Can you figure out how this clock grille was designed?

Can you use a similar idea to make grilles in the shape of a triangle, pentagon, hexagon, or octagon? It is "as easy as pie."

ANSWER: The clock grille was based on the idea of slicing up a pie into 12 parts. On a separate piece of cardboard, cut out a pie slice that will be exactly one twelfth of the whole circle. If each message is going to be eight letters long, punch out eight holes in the pie slice, or template, like this (next page):

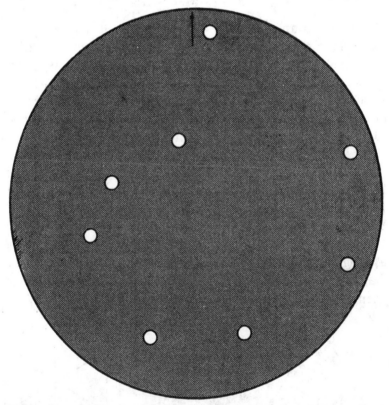

Place this grille with the arrow pointing to the hour of your birth on the circle of letters on page 50, for a one-word description of your character.

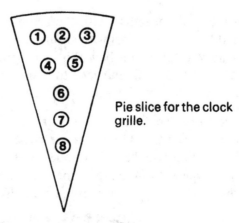

Pie slice for the clock grille.

You now want to punch out eight holes in the big grille. Place the pie slice over any hourly position on the big grille and punch out any hole you want. For example, you may place the slice between the 1 o'clock and 2 o'clock positions and punch out hole No. 1; place it between the 3 and 4 o'clock positions and punch out hole No. 2; place it between the 10 and 11 o'clock positions and punch out hole No. 7; and so on.

When the grille is completed, place it over a blank circle. Put it in the 1 o'clock position and write a message through the holes; then do the same with the other hours. The grille must have an arrow on it to point to the 12 hourly positions on the big circle.

The "slice of pie" idea can be used for grilles of other shapes, as long as the sides and angles of the grille are all equal. The diagrams below show how the slices of pie would look in a triangle and in a hexagon.

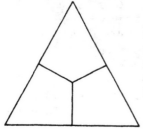

On the left, a pie slice for an equilateral triangle. On the right, a pie slice for a regular hexagon.

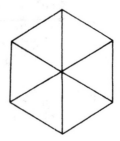

Ricky's Star is a development of the hexagon, with an extra triangle added to each edge for the points of the star. As given here, it allows six 12-letter messages, or a long message of 72 letters. The letters are entered clockwise, first in the points of the star, then continuing the spiral through the inside of the star. The slice of pie is in the shape of a diamond (two equilateral triangles put together). Two holes are punched in each slice, one in the point section and one on the inside of the hexagon.

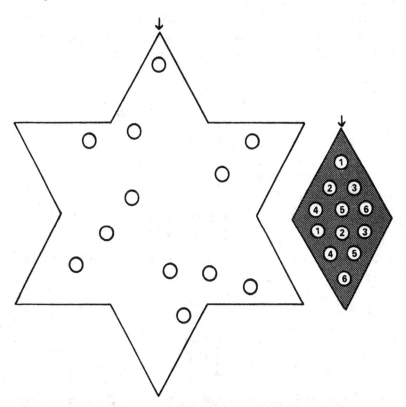

Ricky's Star and its "pie slice"—here a diamond. Punch out one number in the upper half of the diamond and the same number in the lower half, when you place the diamond in different positions on the star.

THE NEW MATH

Computers take alphabetical information, turn it into numbers, and store it away. Why not reverse the process, and turn numbers into letters? We can, and do, in a popular and interesting type of puzzle.

Any type of mathematical calculation can be used, though long division usually makes the most entertaining puzzles. But let us begin with an easy multiplication problem:

$$
\begin{array}{r}
9\ 7\ 2 \\
2\ 1 \\
\hline
9\ 7\ 2 \\
1\ 9\ 4\ 4 \\
\hline
2\ 0\ 4\ 1\ 2
\end{array}
$$

Scramble the first ten letters of the alphabet (omitting I to avoid confusing it with 1) in any fashion:

$$
\begin{array}{cccccccccc}
1 & 2 & 3 & 4 & 5 & 6 & 7 & 8 & 9 & 0 \\
C & K & A & G & J & E & H & B & F & D
\end{array}
$$

Then for each digit in the problem, substitute the appropriate letter of the alphabet:

$$
\begin{array}{r}
F\ H\ K \\
K\ C \\
\hline
F\ H\ K \\
C\ F\ G\ G \\
\hline
K\ D\ G\ C\ K
\end{array}
$$

This one is really not very difficult to solve. Because the first and third lines are the same, C (on the second line) must be 1. K, beginning the last line, must be 1 larger than C, since it is not C, so it is 2. K × K = G, so G must be 4. The rest is simple.

Try your problem on a few puzzle-minded friends, and if they find it neither too hard nor too easy, add it to your collection. If you desire, you may use letters which give some kind of message. Using all five lines would be too difficult, so try to write a message on the first, second, and fifth lines. Put spaces for the digits on these three lines, and insert some sort of symbol to show where digits are repeated.

```
— — —                    -  - #
    — —                      # %
— — — — —          #  -  - % #
```

Now try to write a message which repeats the same letter wherever the symbol is repeated; the remaining dashes must be filled with all different letters. The message might be, "Ban no nylon." Perhaps you can do better. Fill all the letters you have found into your complete problem, choosing additional letters at random for lines three and four, if they are needed.

Here are some problems for you to try to solve:

1. P I P
    D I D
    P E E K

2. B E S S E
    G A G S
    B A S S

3. A T E
    A T
    Y E M S
    E L S
    T I M S

4. I R A
    A T
    E E E
    P Q Q A
    P E A C E

5. B U S
    I S
    I I L E
    B U S
    L A T E

6. T O M
    T O O L G A
    M T
    B O G
    B M O
    B R A
    B R A

<pre>
7.   M A N   8.   R A N
   O N │ T E A M   O N │ D I M E
         O N   R A
         O T A   O O M
         O J O   O O R
           O L M   H E
           O L M   H E

9.   A I D   10.   B A R
   I N │ P L A N   T O │ S P O R T
         D P   S B O
         B A A   S I R
         B L A   O F
           A L N   T U T
           A L N   T U T
</pre>

ANSWERS:

1. $151 + 858$	6. $6890 \div 26$
2. $10550 - 9295$	7. $5481 \div 29$
3. 265×26	8. $3976 \div 14$
4. 296×63	9. $8024 \div 34$
5. 284×14	10. $17892 \div 28$

DAD'S CHALLENGE

La Guillotine

Mr. Bennett was a puzzle nut, and a lot of it had rubbed off on his son, George. Whenever one of them had something to fool the other, he was eager to show it off. George thought he had something when he brought the following table home from school:

```
    1 2 3 4 5
1 │ A B C D E
2 │ F G H I J
3 │ K L MN O
4 │ P Q R S T
5 │ U V WX Y
```

"Ever see anything like this before?" he asked.

"Hm—yes, it looks like something we used to call Checkerboard. It was used to write a message using only five different symbols. The numbers for T would be 4 and 5, so you would use your fourth and fifth symbols together to represent T."

"No, this is something different. It is called La Guillotine, and it was used by the resistance movement during the Second World War. You remember that Germany defeated France, and for a while part of France was occupied and part wasn't?"

"I believe I heard my great-grandfather remark something about it," said Mr. Bennett dryly.

"Let me show you how it works. I want to write the message, 'Patrol is quiet,' so I'll copy down the message and put the proper number below each letter."

```
P   A   T   R   O   L   I   S   Q   U   I   E   T
41  11  45  43  35  32  24  44  42  51  24  15  45
```

"Is that all? That would be very easy."

"No, there is another step. Now you take each figure and substitute some letter of the alphabet that appears on that line. The first figure is 4, so I could choose P, Q, R, S, or T. The next figure is 1, so I could choose A, B, C, D, or E. I wrote the message like this."

PB CB RY TM OU NF FQ SR QI UD GQ AY SX

"That's better, but probably not too difficult, even so."

"No, but this was unoccupied France, and the Germans weren't there, and the French government was disorganized. It was good enough then. You could change the table, of course, and you wouldn't *show* that there were two letters in a group."

"Those letters you selected, suppose I—"

"Just play along, Dad. Do you think you would have much trouble reading it?"

"I shouldn't think so."

"Let me show you, anyway. You take each letter in the message, find it on the table, and substitute the figure at the top of the column. Like this."

PB CB RY TM OU NF FQ SR QI UD GQ AY SX
12 32 35 53 51 41 12 43 24 14 22 15 44

"Wow!"

"You get it now, Dad? You take each of these two figures, and find out what letter they give you from the table. The message now reads: 'Blow up bridges.' "

"That's great, George. It might not fool people too long, but it could have its purposes. If the French police intercepted the messenger, he could show them how to read it one way, but if it got through to the resistance movement, they would know enough to read it the other way. Let me see how you wrote the message."

On his paper George had it all written out:

```
P   A   T   R   O   L   I   S   Q   U   I   E   T
41  11  45  43  35  32  24  44  42  51  24  15  45
B   L   O   W   U   P   B   R   I   D   G   E   S
12  32  35  53  51  41  12  43  24  14  22  15  44
PB  CB  RY  TM  OU  NF  FQ  SR  QI  UD  GQ  AY  SX
```

The bottom line was found by making substitutions from the two digits above. Thus, 41, reading down, gave P; 12, reading down, gave B; 13 gave C, and so on.

(Variation: One Checkerboard table could be used for changing letters into numbers, and a different Checkerboard for changing numbers back into letters.)

"It makes you wonder, doesn't it," said Mr. Bennett, after he had studied it out, "to whom your loyalty really belongs. Many French thought they ought to support their Vichy government, and others thought they should support the refugee government in London. Which ones were really traitors?"

"Gee, Dad, if they didn't know which government to support, maybe they should have written their messages so the same answer would come out no matter which way you read it."

His father gave him a strange look.

Playfair

"Your code reminds me of something the British army used during the First World War called Playfair. Simple to use and able to be varied quickly, it really isn't very safe—probably only an hour's security—but usually that was enough for a field cipher. The order would be given and carried out, and after that, who cared whether the Germans broke it or not?"

```
V   I   C   T   O
R   Y   A   B   D
E   F   G   H   J
K   L   M   N   P
Q   S   U   W   X
```

"It was written two letters at a time. If you wanted to write VG, you would imagine that these two letters formed a rectangle inside the larger square, and you would use the other two corners, CE. LO would be written PI. If the two letters were on the same line, you would use the letters following: EG would be FH. If the two letters were in the same column, you would use the letters beneath: UG would be CM. You had to be careful not to use double letters, because these were too much of a giveaway, and you would break them apart by putting an X between them, before enciphering the message."

He wrote a practice message:

BE TX TE RD AY SA RE CO MI NG
RH OW VH YR BA UY EK TV LC MH

With very little practice, George found he could read it easily.

"Then, after an hour or so, I suppose they would make up a new alphabet table, based on a different key word. The letters could even be entered diagonally, or something like that. How would you go about breaking this, Dad?"

"Getting started is the hardest part. But once you have made a good start, the letters are so strongly interrelated that the whole thing falls apart. What you try to do is to reconstruct the table. TH is the most common bigram, and if you can find how that is written, you are off flying. Or you might imagine a familiar word in the message, such as a name. Some words are giveaways. Suppose you wanted to write 'Bennett.' If the letters were coupled like this, –B EN NE TX T–, you have EN and NE. If EN is written HK, then NE would be written just the opposite, KH. Many words have the same bigram repeated, or the reverse bigram." He wrote:

TH IR TE EN TH
BA NA NA or –B AN AN A–
–F OR TH WI TH
CH UR CH
MI MI C–

```
NO ON
–L  ET  TE  R–
RE  ME  MB  ER  or  –R  EM  EM  BE  R–
```

"By GE OR GE," George exclaimed. "I guess you should be careful never to write anything about bananas. That gets repeated no matter how it is divided."

He thought a moment. "You didn't say anything about using this during the Second World War, Dad."

"No, things had moved pretty far ahead by then. I remember a story from ancient times, when a king wanted to send a secret message. He shaved off the hair of a slave's head, had the message tattooed, then when the slave's hair grew out again, sent him on his way."

"Man, a modern war could be all over by then."

"Simple ciphers were often very effective during the American Civil War, too. Not very many messages were intercepted, and when they were, usually you knew about it. But the coming of radio changed all that. The material comes in floods. Any message sent by radio may have been picked off by the enemy.

"During the Second World War, both sides used ciphering machines made in Sweden. These machines were supposed to be safe for a couple of days to a week. I doubt if that would be true today, with the development of computers. Anyway, the settings on the machines were changed every day, and if the ciphers were ever broken within that time, no one is talking."

Gemini

Two days later George brought a paper home from school and excitedly showed it to his father.

"I told my math teacher about Playfair and he had me demonstrate it to the class. Then today he brought this table, called Gemini, and gave a copy to everybody in the class. It works like Playfair, substituting two letters at a time, but it is a lot more difficult to break.

"It's very simple to use. If you want to write TH, you find T

61

Gemini

	A	B	C	D	E	F	G	H	I	J	K	L	M	N	O	P	Q	R	S	T	U	V	W	X	Y	Z
A	KF	DC	RV	BJ	WM	SE	GI	PT	HS	IL	VY	TW	LQ	OG	QG	EA	ZU	CD	FZ	XR	NK	UX	MN	QB	JP	YH
B	TL	ZW	UY	JN	FC	DI	HG	KX	WE	AD	YO	VK	ET	RZ	MH	VT	IM	GV	NB	OR	QU	SS	XF	CQ	PA	LJ
C	DZ	VL	FN	AR	SH	WU	KK	EC	PF	ZA	OJ	QI	UW	MG	HU	RQ	BX	YV	JT	HP	GY	IE	NS	TM	LD	XB
D	WL	QS	AB	HZ	YU	ID	LC	ZR	BF	FW	TI	NT	KY	GN	XX	YF	OV	VO	PE	EQ	JH	RG	UK	MJ	SM	CA
E	AP	PD	CH	SO	MZ	OB	YY	VJ	ZQ	LW	FR	UC	NG	UU	QL	TK	DT	HF	IX	BM	KI	XS	WA	JV	RU	GE
F	PN	IC	BE	VX	KM	MF	ND	GP	RW	XI	HA	JU	ZV	CC	WT	SZ	UR	EK	YG	RS	LT	PQ	BR	QM	QQ	AS
G	YB	UI	VW	NA	EZ	XD	TJ	MP	AG	IP	BG	HV	IY	ZF	OK	DN	KE	FH	SC	JL	TV	GJ	QM	CU	ZC	WO
H	FK	MX	LH	OZ	JE	ER	UP	FT	LU	NZ	PX	DU	VB	XY	HU	VC	HH	SB	AI	KS	CO	XW	SQ	CT	UM	DD
I	OM	KD	FB	DF	CV	VR	BQ	WG	ZY	RO	ZL	PB	YA	QN	CT	VO	RI	WW	SB	QA	CO	TE	YN	XY	ES	JO
J	SL	OT	TO	RN	HE	QJ	MI	DU	VB	WF	NC	GR	XH	BD	IZ	AY	PP	ZM	KV	CS	FL	EX	LG	SK	GK	UQ
K	ZI	NJ	OY	IB	GO	AA	VF	SR	EU	RL	CG	WD	FE	PR	LP	XV	YQ	QX	HT	UZ	MW	JS	TC	BH	DM	PK
L	WY	RH	DG	CY	PV	ZP	JW	HC	UB	BZ	MK	FX	WN	VE	TR	KO	AM	XL	SU	GT	II	NQ	EJ	YD	OS	QF

M	SJ	XC	QR	OI	OL	FF	CN	BO	JG	DX	LK	IS	TP	AW	NI	GH	WQ	RY	VV	YM	ZT	PZ	KU	HB	UA	EE
N	GD	BS	JK	FG	XQ	HY	EM	QE	MO	KB	AU	YR	SA	UT	PI	TZ	LV	TN	CW	DL	RC	WX	ZH	OF	VZ	IJ
O	XZ	EF	WH	YS	ZJ	NX	AN	UL	MD	CK	GM	ME	IA	TU	FV	QO	VP	BT	LY	JB	SW	DQ	PG	RR	KC	HD
P	BY	HJ	SX	EB	DS	CI	OW	WP	NO	YL	KZ	XT	QC	FA	UN	GU	KN	ZG	AH	VM	LE	RF	IK	TD	MV	
Q	IT	AX	PM	XA	NH	LZ	AO	TQ	CL	JF	US	EO	GW	HN	OP	WI	FY	MC	DB	RE	BU	YJ	VD	KR	ZK	SV
R	VH	SG	NU	ZZ	QT	PW	DV	LB	IQ	UF	XO	KJ	XN	JD	HL	YE	CP	OX	GS	TA	EY	AC	FI	WK	MR	BN
S	NM	IR	GQ	UO	AF	TG	RB	CE	YT	MA	JX	JA	DY	ZN	ED	VI	HW	KH	BV	WJ	LS	QZ	OU	PC	XK	FP
T	RT	YI	KW	PY	IV	UE	SF	XJ	DK	GG	EP	BA	CX	NR	JC	MM	QH	LO	WB	ZD	ON	HQ	AL	VS	FU	NP
U	MY	LI	EL	WR	TF	RJ	XE	YP	GB	VA	DW	OH	HX	PO	SD	IG	JZ	FQ	QK	NN	EN	ZS	CM	AV	BC	KT
V	UJ	JI	HO	QW	LN	KG	ZE	RA	SP	EH	BL	CB	PU	YZ	DR	OQ	IF	TX	BP	WV	MS	GC	FD	AK	NY	
W	EW	TS	YK	KL	BI	JJ	IN	OC	QP	ST	RX	DA	AE	LM	GZ	PH	MQ	UD	XG	FO	CF	VU	HR	NV	LA	ZB
X	QD	CZ	MB	GF	UG	BW	WS	JM	FJ	TH	SY	LR	VQ	RM	ZX	NE	AT	EV	PL	YC	KP	IU	DO	HI	OA	
Y	HM	GA	XU	LX	RP	DP	FS	AZ	TB	QV	WC	PJ	MT	IW	BK	UH	KQ	NL	OD	SI	DE	CR	JY	ZO	EG	VN
Z	CJ	WZ	GX	TT	VG	GL	PS	NW	KA	OE	QY	HK	JR	SN	YX	LF	EI	DH	UV	MU	AQ	FM	BB	XP	IO	RD

in the column to the left, and H in the line across the top, and they meet at XJ. Then when you want to read a message, you look for X in the left column, and J above, and they meet at TH. It's reciprocal."

As his father studied the paper, George continued: "My teacher said you could use it like ordinary Vigenère if you wanted to, by just ignoring the second letter in each pair—only that kind of Vigenère wouldn't be reciprocal."

He waited a few minutes, then said, "Isn't it great, Dad?"

"I'll buy that. How many kids got copies?"

"About forty."

"And you don't know where your teacher got it?"

"From a book, I guess."

"Then I'd say it wasn't very much of a secret. Spies from every country in the world could have it by now."

George's face fell. "Then the codes you get out of a book aren't much good, are they?"

"Oh, I didn't say that. Usually they are given in their simplest form, and you can think of a way to vary them so they are still secret and effective. I'm sure that I can think of some other ways to use this table."

That evening Mr. Bennett had several messages ready for his son. The first one was:

FX LQ FZ CD UU JB WT PO BF SA TU FZ IV IQ IX

Of course the first thing George did was to try to use the table in the way he had been taught. FX gave him LL, which was very discouraging. "Lots of words end in LL," he mused. "You didn't write the message in reverse, did you, Dad?"

"No, I wouldn't play a trick like that on my only son and heir."

"How much time do I get?"

"Just one sitting. When you give up, that's it."

Mr. Bennett turned his attention to the newspaper, and George busied himself with paper and pencil for five minutes.

Suddenly he let out a scream that brought his mother running in from the kitchen. When she realized this was just father-and-son stuff, she smiled and retreated.

"I've got it, Dad. I almost gave up too easily. You just read this in the regular way. I didn't think there would be a word beginning LL, but I forgot about llamas."

He was ready to tackle another. This one read:

EJ OK LO ZI NQ

Again George tried it in the normal way, being careful to write out the whole puzzle, but it didn't seem to work. His father seemed engrossed in the newspaper, but was getting a good deal of amusement peeking out over the top at his son's many expressions of puzzlement. But his effort was rewarded.

"Nothing to it," George bragged a little. "You just have to change the letters around. EJ is really JE. After that you read the message with the table."

"Then what took you so long?" his father remarked. "I just took pity on you. Remember, I could have reversed at the beginning instead of at the end, or, if there was a middle step, I could have reversed then. But to make things easier, I won't use that idea of reversing again."

"How many more, Dad?"

"I have four more. I did think of an idea for using the table with a key letter, but it was complicated, and I didn't want to take advantage of you. I think you'll find this next one hard enough."

SS KR RC SA AI OI VP ZW UQ

The first attempt to solve it did not seem to work. George wondered what to do next. There seemed to be an extra step involved, but he didn't know what to do. SS gave him BV, but when he tried BV it just gave him SS again, so that didn't help. Finally he was ready for a hint.

"I didn't get it, Dad, but I think maybe you use the table twice. Am I right?"

"You could be," said his father, noncommittally.

"But how could I use it again?" He was talking half to himself. "Say, wait. I could divide these letters the other way—remember 'banana'—and use the table again."

So he read the cipher letters with the table, divided them the other way, and tried to read them again with the table, but it didn't work out.

"It's got me stumped, Dad," he finally admitted.

"Too bad, when you were so close. You had the right idea, but you did things in the wrong order. When I wrote the message, I first used the table, then re-divided the letters, and used the table again."

MA	RK	TH	EP	AS	SI	NG	HO	UR
SJ	XO	XJ	TK	FZ	YT	EM	VC	FQ
S	JX	OX	JT	KF	ZY	TE	MV	CF	Q
S	SK	RR	CS	AA	IO	IV	PZ	WU	Q

"You would have had to do exactly the opposite. You should begin with the last line on this paper, then work to the line above, then to the line above that, and finally the message."

"You could have made it even harder, couldn't you? You could keep on dividing, and substituting, and dividing again, and substituting again, as long as you wanted to." George was fascinated.

"You could, but it's a lot of work, and all of us being human, too many errors would creep in."

"Well, try me again, Dad. I'm fresh as a daisy."

The next message read:

BOM QNR JTL TJD JFD

"Three letters in a group. Is that important, Dad?"

"Just a little hint I threw in free. I wouldn't give it to the Nazis, but I would to you."

George tried to read just two of the letters in each group, thinking perhaps the third letter was either a null or a true letter, but it didn't work out. He decided that once again it must be necessary to use the table twice, but somehow he couldn't pull the thing off.

His father showed him how the message was written:

WE ARE NOT ALONE

WEA REN OTA LON EXX

BI   QT   JB   TR   JV

OM   NR   TL   JD   FD

BOM QNR JTL TJD JFD

"The third line you get by enciphering the two letters immediately above. The fourth line is trickier. You use IA to get OM, and TN to get NR. In reading the message, of course, you start with the bottom line and work back to the preceding line."

"One more, Dad," said George doggedly.

"Coming right up, and to give you a clue, I'll tell you exactly how I wrote the message, and your problem is to read it. I took the sets of letters in my original message and substituted with the table. But, instead of using that particular substitution, I used the bigram immediately below it on the table. Thus, AT would normally give XR, but I used the letters below, OR. See how kind I was to you? Instead of using the one right below, I could have used the one five lines below, or ten to the right, or 15 on a diagonal."

The message was written:

YP BE ZM JH DK XJ EK UR

George fiddled with it, and fiddled with it, but somehow it wouldn't come out right.

"It is sneaky," his father agreed. "Here is how to read it: YP, the first message bigram, is changed to UH, and when you read UH it gives YP, but now you are in the right position on the table, and the bigram above it is XJ. Reading XJ gives you TH. The message reads, 'The circus is hereq.'

"But there is a short cut, if you don't mind figuring a little. First try to read the couplets in the normal way. YP gives UH. The second letter is a true letter (because when I wrote the message, I stayed in the correct vertical column). The first letter will be one letter off (because I moved down an extra row when writing the message), and you will substitute the preceding letter of the alphabet."

YP	BE	ZM	JH	DK	XJ	EK	UR
UH	FC	JR	DU	TI	TH	FR	FQ
T	E	I	C	S	S	E	E
TH	EC	IR	CU	SI	SH	ER	EQ

"Last one," said George firmly. "I have to get this one."
"And I want to help you, so I made it easy."

SC QO CQ VA GA EP ER DT HH KK IX DZ TA KI CD ZT

It didn't take George very long. He read the message with the table, and it came out:

GQ OP BX UJ YB TK HF EQ IP CG ES CA RT EU AR MU

"Too easy, Dad. Just read the first letters and forget the second letters."

"Well, what about all those letters you didn't use in the last message? I think you'd better sit down and read what they say."

QP XJ BK FQ PG SA TU RU

FINGERPRINTED WORDS

The class had recently read the Sherlock Holmes story, "The Adventure of the Dancing Men," and Mr. Hunter, the teacher, wondered if anyone in the class could break a simple substitution code. He placed a message on the board:

TODODJOT KM JTQNP ZMET KORKJMMCB KMDMTTMH

The class began to work furiously. Marilyn, a good student, had come prepared. She had no idea what the message was about and she had no idea what substitution table Mr. Hunter had used. But she looked something up in a little book she had brought, worked quickly, and in a couple of minutes raised her hand.

"The message reads, 'Remember to bring your textbooks tomorrow.' "

The other pupils in the class looked on in amazement. They had been carefully counting the number of times each letter was used and were going to call the most-used letter E. That would not have worked in this particular message anyway.

"Would you mind telling us how you worked it out so quickly?" Mr. Hunter asked.

Marilyn did. The class was surprised and some of the poor losers said she had no right to look in a book.

How did she break the code so quickly?

ANSWER: Many words, especially long ones, use repeated letters. Sometimes several letters are repeated, and the pattern is different for almost every word. If you number the words according to their letters, they look like this:

```
R E ME MB E R        T O MO R R O W
1 2 3 2 3 4 2 1      1 2 3 2 4 4 2 5
```

Marilyn's code book contained lists of these "fingerprinted words," arranged according to numbers. By looking up these numbers, she easily identified REMEMBER and TOMOR-ROW, and after decoding these words she was able to decode the rest of the message quickly.

A Short List

You may want to build up your own list of fingerprinted words. Here is a beginning. Keep the words on file cards or on a box of old business cards.

These words also make an entertaining game. Give your friends a number pattern and see if they can guess the word. They may need some clues to help them!

121123	mammal, pepper	1221345634	illiterate
121133	tattoo	122312	arrear
12113424	lollipop	1223142	attract
121134245	poppycock	122322	assess, boohoo, hoodoo, voodoo
1213143152	initiation		
1213345	opossum	122323	needed
12134134	nonsense	122324154	assistant
121342345	ninetieth	122334	woolly
121343115	evergreen	12233445678	bookkeeping
12134331	nineteen	12234115	offshoot
1213434	ukulele	12234155	eggshell
122121	deeded	1223415536	Appomattox
12212234	assassin	122341563	immediate
122123	inning	1223421	reenter
122133	appall	12234223	cookbook
12213435	irritate, opponent	12234225	poolroom

12234255	heedless, needless	12323421	remember
122343225	footstool	1232344	oneness
1223435163	accelerate	12324213	cataract
122344	abbess	123243215	paragraph
12234435167	accom-modate	12324425	tomorrow
122344546	innkeeper	123245224	seventeen
1223445625	occurrence	12324545	Honolulu
122345221	foolproof	1233214546	millimeter
12234543	appetite	12332332442	Mississippi
1223455	address, illness, oppress	1233234	baggage
		12332425566	Tallahassee
12234566	goodness	123324422	Tennessee
1231142	trotter	1233411	success
12311451	scissors	123342335	hillbilly
12312	Miami	1233432	freezer
1231231	alfalfa	1233432311	sleeveless
1231233452	Cincinnati	1233433	possess
123124211	senseless	123344	coffee
1231243	retreat	1233445	balloon, bassoon, raccoon
1231244	newness, repress	12334511	suppress
1231421	Atlanta	12334514	commerce
1231423	prepare	1233455	goddess
1231441531	excellence	1233455426	commission
123145235	incidence	12334556	ballroom, killdeer
1232122	referee	123345566	committee
1232141	minimum	12334562784714	correspond-ence
1232142	reserve, reverse	1233456311	speechless, sleepiness

12334566	mattress, misspell
12341254	instinct
12341255	baseball, neatness
123413152	intuition
123413512	thirtieth
12342124	rendered
1234223	monsoon
1234233	dismiss
12342332	bandanna
12342543	moreover
1234314	opinion
12343525	seafarer
12343553	Cheyenne
12344315	omission
1234432	dresser

12344325	staccato
12344341	grinning
12344355	openness
12344356673	Chattanooga
123445561377	whippoor-will
123445667	classroom
12344567782	grasshopper
12345321	revolver
123453511	sorceress
123454234264	independ-ence
123455453	beginning
123455466	embarrass
12345651247	participate
123456575623	constitution

PARTY WORD GAMES

The numbers in the following stories are a code for certain words. Each group of numbers gives the pattern of the secret word. See how clever you are by figuring out the correct words. (Answers begin on page 96, but no fair peeking!)

Three-Letter Patterns

122 was saving for a trip to the farm, but when she came to 122 up her money, she could not 121 it out. However, her 121 offered to help her, on condition that she 121 not tell 121. "121 is the word," he cautioned her.

On the 121 of her arrival, she stopped at an 122. Nearby was a golf course, and watching the players 122 122, she wondered how they could afford the 122. One player was a 121 and she saw him 121 the ball into a trap. She looked for other guests, but there were none there except a 121, who complained of feeling 122 and went to bed early. Afraid that someone would say 122 to her, she, 122, retired early.

The next morning she arrived at the farm. "122," she thought, "it is just like being at a 122." She could hear the 122 of the doves and the 122 of the cows. Out of the corner of her 121 she could see a 122, and she dodged. She stooped to pet the 121 with his silly 121 tail, until he chased the cat, which ran for a while but then turned and scratched him. "That's 121 for 121," she thought.

The farmer was busy feeding the baby. She thought it 122 that he tied a 121 around the 121 and fed him his 122, which seemed to 121 him. When the baby started to cry, the farmer said, "121, 121, little one." He gave her some cherries, and she politely placed each 121 on her plate.

Outside, she saw a 121 with her 122 lamb. "121!" she exclaimed. She tried to 122 the lamb but it was full of 121. It ran off to the 122 side of the barn and said "122" at her.

"112!" she screamed, when she thought she saw a snake.

"It is only an 112," the farmer told her.

"121?" she returned in surprise.

"To 122 is human. Have a ride in my 121."

Everything was 122 right, and 121 the day began to 122, she was glad she had come.

Four-Letter Patterns

A boy named 1221 and a girl named 1221 liked to meet at 1221. During the 1211 after lunch, they would 1211 on the lawn, playing with a 12-12 while her 1212 and 1212 would 1221 out at them and 1123 kindness. They liked him because he did not 1211 them and was livelier than a 1212 bird. Then when he heard the whistles 1221, he would jump up and hurry off to do his daily good 1221.

Five-Letter Patterns

Bobby asked his 12113 if he could go camping in his 12322.

"Very well," she agreed, "but wash yourself and attend to your 12213. There is 12213 powder on the shelf."

He invited his friend, Rollo, a boy with a lot of 12312, to come along. They set up camp at a 12321 spot. It was 11231 out in the woods at night, but Bobby was not a 12113 who was afraid of everything. He heard the sound of a 12113 goat, and wondered if it might be that 12131 animal, a 11232.

"If you think that, you're a 12113," said Rollo.

"It was only an 12232," said Bobby quaveringly, his cheeks 12123.

He spent a wakeful night, while Rollo slept like a 12113 in a museum. In the morning a flock of 12232 flew over. He heard a 12113 bluejay, while a mockingbird tried to 12123 it.

When he left the tent, he was drenched with water for Rollo

had made a 12213 trap. He found that Rollo had brought nothing but an 12312 to eat, which was not exactly 12332 from heaven. He longed for a cup of hot 12123.

Picking a wild 12113 to take home to his mother, he made up the 12332 (also known as a 12321) that it is better to camp with your 12113 than with a friend.

One, Two, Three

Can you think of six words with the pattern 123123?
Can you think of a word with the pattern 12341234?

Animals

1.	Songbird	1 2 3 4 5 2 1 3 6 7 8
2.	Sea mammal	1 2 3 1 2 4 5 6
3.	Busy on Christmas	1 2 3 4 5 2 2 1
4.	Poisonous reptile	1 2 3 3 4 5 6 7 2 8 5
5.	Spider	1 2 3 2 4 1 5 6 2
6.	A type of dog	1 2 3 3 4 2 3
7.	A red-headed bird	1 2 2 3 4 5 6 7 5 8
8.	A dead body	1 2 3 1 2 4 4
9.	A fuzzy larva	1 2 3 4 5 6 7 8 8 2 5
10.	An insect's sleeping room	1 2 1 2 2 3
11.	Dines on insects	1 2 3 4 1 3 4 5
12.	Wears a coat of arms	1 2 3 1 4 5 6 6 7
13.	A large ape	1 2 1 3 3 4
14.	A dangerous fish	1 2 3 3 2 4 5 6 2
15.	An extinct mammal	1 2 1 1 3 4 5
16.	A stinging insect	1 2 3 1 4 5 1 5 5
17.	Songbird	1 2 3 1 4 5 6 7 7
18.	A breed of dog	1 2 3 2 4 5 2 4 5
19.	A small ape	1 2 3 4 5 6 7 8 9 9
20.	Wanted for its fur	1 2 3 4 1 2 3 5 5 6
21.	A singing insect	1 2 1 3 4 3
22.	A household pest	1 2 1 3 4 2 5 1 6
23.	A reptile with legs	1 2 3 1 3 4 5 6 7
24.	Big and fat	1 2 3 3 4 3 4 5 6 7 8 9
25.	Do not touch	1 2 3 4 2 1 5 4
26.	Likes to jump	1 2 3 4 2 5 6 6

CRYPTIC TREASURE HUNTS

The First Method

Do you have a lot of puzzle-minded friends? Then why not give a party for them, featuring a treasure hunt? The hunt described here involves hiding short messages, each one giving a clue to the location of the next message. Now where should the messages be hidden?

1. Hand the first clue to each guest in turn to direct them to the place where the next clue is hidden. If you have a "welcome" mat, the second clue might be hidden under it. But do not just say, "Look under the welcome mat." Make the clue a little more cryptic than that, such as: GLAD YOU COULD COME.

2. If you have a dog, you could hide the third clue under his dish or bed. Then the second clue would read: WHERE THE BURGLAR ALARM MIGHT BE. (A dog is a sort of burglar alarm, right?)

3. ALWAYS EMPTY ON A HOLIDAY directs the players to the mailbox.

4. A GOOD PLACE TO BATHE TWINS leads to the twin laundry tubs.

5. THE PLACE WHERE GLOVES ARE KEPT means the glove compartment in a car.

6. WHAT WOULD HAPPEN TO US IF THIS STOPPED? should lead your guests to the world globe.

7. PAUSE A MOMENT AND REFLECT tells them to look near the mirror.

8. TWO MOUTHS TO MATCH YOUR EARS must refer to the stereo speakers.

9. A SHARP PERSON WILL KEEP HIS DISTANCE from the cactus plant.

10. THE BEST PLACE FOR A WRECK leads them to a prominent spot in the recreation room. (Rec. room, ok?)

11. ISLAND WHERE THE TREASURE WAS FOUND means the next clue will be found inside the cover of the book *Treasure Island*.

12. PLACE OF PERPETUAL WINTER leads them to the freezer. And here is where you have hidden the prize.

The Second Method

The first method might be too simple for your friends, who are pretty sharp and want a full evening of fun with puzzles. Be a rascal and turn each of the 12 previous messages into code.

1. The first clue can serve the double purpose of pairing off the guests and directing them to the welcome mat. If you expect 12 guests, prepare 12 messages in the following way:

Set A				Set B			
HEAZM	QQNMK	TYPHG	Z	NNQKV	EGJFK	KLQJI	E
ESLTH	VTEOL	KGSHX	R	FLMTY	UBWNJ	TXAJS	I
ZNLDM	KAGHJ	TNKEM	T	GEMHV	CEBJL	KMOQK	M
OSTUI	VMQLB	RVOPP	J	ALXST	UZPXT	QRKDJ	D
JUJNT	XRQIO	SKDOC	Z	YJIMI	LFPBV	LZFNR	E
KQPXM	QIMXN	POMJK	S	WRKGV	EWRLU	HPRHM	P

The letters in Set A are pure random letters, pulled out of the air. To find the letters in Set B, copy down the letters in Set A, and below it write the hidden meaning:

H E A Z M Q Q N M K T Y P H G Z
G L A D Y O U C O U L D C O M E

Refer to the Rogues' Gallery, and use this table to combine letters, in the manner described on page 15:

N N Q K V E G . . .

Do the same for the other five sets of letters in Set A, and the results will be Set B. Cut out these 12 messages, drop them in a bowl, and have each guest draw one. If you want to pair a boy with a girl, put the messages from Set A in one bowl and those from Set B in another. The boys should draw from one bowl and the girls from the other.

Give a copy of the Rogues' Gallery to each guest so they can try to pair off. When the right partners combine their letters, the decoded message will be sensible.

2. The next message, which the players will find under the doormat, might read: BE MIGHT ALARM BURGLAR THE WHERE. This is a simple reversal of words. Too easy? This is just the beginning.

3. SYAWLA YTPME NO A YADILOH. Each word is simply read in reverse. Now the hard part begins. You might not want to go any further than this. But a keen group might be anxious for the codes to get harder.

4. SNIWT EHTAB OTECA LPDOO GA. Read the message from the end.

5. THEPL HWECA EREGL ASEVO REKEP T. Reverse the letters in the second and fourth groups; read from the front.

6. WHATW HULDO NPPEA IOUST STHIF PTOPS DE. Exchange first and last letters in each group; read from the front.

7. ARPUI AFTUX LSIRE TOAMU MFTOT EMOQE RLNII TOOAL SNIED OPRIE EFFFI ELODE ACCUI T. Read every third letter.

8. TOOTSO ACYUER SAROHT MTHUMW. Read alternately a letter from the beginning and one from the end.

9. EASHA TRPPE ARSON OWILL NKEEP IHISD RISTA SNCE. Cross out the first letter in each group and read straight through from the beginning.

10. KKCOE RRUWI AARUO TFIEA CPAQL LPATU SJEFB TESHU T. Read every other letter, starting from the end.

11. IDERRF SWTEEO LHHAWU AEESAN NRTUSD. Read all the first letters, then all the second letters, and so on.

12. OKZBD NE ODQODSTZK VHMSDQ. This is the simplest form of Caesar's alphabet. Substitute the letter in the alphabet that follows each letter in the message.

PROBLEMS FOR A MATH CLASS

Suppose some lazy student (not you, of course) didn't finish his math homework. It wasn't his fault; there was a television program he had to watch, or unexpected visitors, or he fell asleep and his mother never woke him up, or . . . Now here's a secret: All math teachers like puzzles, or else they are in the wrong job. If he could just get the teacher interested in a puzzle, mightn't the teacher forget to ask for the homework?

You won't really be fooling the teacher, because he was young once and tried all these tricks himself. But if it is a puzzle he hasn't heard before, he might forgive you anyway. Here are some you might try. Answers begin on page 98.

Einstein's Dream

Read the following message:

565 099 131 862 010 576 230

Watson's Needle

Can you demonstrate to the class how an IBM punch card is read?

Great Caesar

The famous Julius Caesar proclaimed one of his famous victories with the famous words, "Veni, vidi, vici." If he had written the words instead, he would probably have used code, and the code he would likely have used has become known as Caesar's alphabet. It consists simply of substituting for each letter another letter appearing a given number of positions further down the alphabet. If the key number was 3, and our alphabet was used, the message would have been written:

V E N I V I D I V I C I
W
X
Y H Q L Y L G L Y L F L

If you had received the bottom line as a message, but did not know the key number, could you have broken it? Do you suppose, on another occasion, perhaps Brutus did?

Orphan Annie

Dr. Infinity, a mad scientist, is planning to blow up the whole universe. Obviously, he must be found quickly. The following message was intercepted from him:

X H T H S A R P A R N Z S O Y H G S E Y O A S X

It is known that he used a kind of Caesar's alphabet, but naturally not the simple one just described. He used it with a transposed alphabet, rather than our straight alphabet, and it is not known how he scrambled his letters, or what key number he used. However, a previous message from him was broken, and on this one he used the following table:

A B C D E F G H I J K L M N O P Q R S T U V WX Y Z
J K D L M N P Q B S U W X Z F V I G C E T A O R H Y

He probably used the same alphabet, but with a different key. From the old table, can you break the new message in time to thwart his vile purposes? Hurry, hurry . . .

Thunder Mountain

Darryll is reading an exciting mystery, in which the solution depends upon solving the following code:

H Q Q D Z N E N R D Z N S Z M O E Y M N

Ted Wilford, the hero of the story, has discovered a clue in the form of an unburned scrap of paper:

			Y	331
			Z	332
R	233		&	333

If you were Ted, could you have broken the code?

Thunder Mountain II

In connection with Thunder Mountain, can you use the following table to construct an unusual variation:

11	12	13	21	22	23	31	32	33
V	I	C	T	O	R	Y	A	B
D	E	F	G	H	J	K	L	M
N	P	Q	S	U	W	X	Z	&

Pig Pen

Can you read the following message:

Although a simple substitution, it is too short to be broken by ordinary methods. However, can you figure out how the alphabet table was constructed?

Wigwam

Read the following message:

81

Metric

Read the following message:

I. D.

How can you identify a transposition cipher?

How can you identify a simple substitution cipher?

How can you identify a Vigenère cipher with a short key word?

Euclid

Read the following message:

PLEYN ROAAI ETVDG PEENH ARMOT

It is based on the idea of constructing a square and filling the letters into the square.

How many different ways can you think of to fill the letters into a square?

What geometrical figures could you use besides a square?

Nihilist

This is a simple cipher which is quite devilish to break. First a key word, such as JAMES, is chosen, and the letters of the message are copied in a square below the key:

J A M E S
P R E P A
R E T O L
E A V E M
O N D A Y
N I G H T

The letters in JAMES are now rearranged according to their order in the alphabet, and the correct column is copied below each key letter:

```
    A E J M S
  J RPPEA
  A EORTL
  M AEEVM
  E NAODY
  S IHNGT
```

The word JAMES has also been written in a column to the left, and this will tell the order in which letters will be taken out. The line beginning with A comes first, then the line beginning with E, and so on. The message is written: EORTL NAODY RPPEA AEEVM IHNGT.

Because this is double transposition, it will usually prove too difficult for amateurs except in very short messages. But there is a short cut available if the same system is used many times, and the opposition can intercept several messages of *exactly the same length*. Suppose the following five messages were intercepted:

1. N C P N E C V S I A O K U S R I I L O E O T E R S
2. T Y L U C A N D C N I S L O C L C Y E T O Y A A E
3. X R T L E R O M O E W E R P P O W H O A E M N E N
4. S S S A R U A P D N J V A E I E B A L I V E L N L
5. N T A Y L I S P T V E S I E I E C I O S T C S N R

Can you read these five messages? It does not matter what method of transposition was used.

Model T

"Oh, I lost my auto-key, I lost my auto-key," moaned Chuck O. Luck at school.

"What auto-key?" asked his friends.

"I can't tell you. It's a secret. Oh, this is terrible. I lost my auto-key."

This was very puzzling to his friends, who knew Chuck did not own a car. Can you figure out what he was talking about?

Scarab

Allan was in a dither. He had to send a code message, right away, to his friend Ferrell. Each had a copy of the Rogues' Gallery, but the trouble was, they had not agreed on a key in advance. How could he manage it?

Vampire

Can you figure out how to use the following table to write messages:

```
   8 3 1 5 0 9 4 6 2 7
   ┌─────────────────────
   │ V I C T O R Y A
 2 │ B D E F G H J K L M
 7 │ N P Q S U W X Z & ?
```

What advantage does this system have over any other method?

Gregg

Can you read the following messages and tell how they were written:

1. Adla a pes o apl kak.
2. Ths ss s ve df fm rs.
3. Tlb g tse u agn.

Noah's Ark

Can you read the following message and tell how it was written:

Canada young comedian withal mead Saturn

Valley of Fear

Can you tell what the following table is used for? It is not used to write messages.

A	1	J	461	S	745
B	66	K	468	T	866
C	119	L	474	U	929
D	216	M	505	V	945
E	270	N	555	W	964
F	312	O	572	X	994
G	356	P	596	Y	995
H	387	Q	689	Z	998
I	424	R	695		

Vixen

Llewellyn received the following message:

$$47\ 32\ 74\ 78\ 24\ 75\ 66\ 46$$

with the clue "The quick brown fox jumps over the lazy dog." With the aid of this clue, can you help him to read the message?

Bacon & Eggs

Can you read the following message using Bacon's alphabet:

TDCUC JWCUP DSQQG UJWTG

Jolly Roger

DDJQA ZOKWD ADLQA QFNO

Can you read the above message using the following table:

A	A–0	F	B–0	K	C–0	P	D–0	U	E–0
B	A–1	G	B–1	L	C–1	Q	D–1	V	E–1
C	A–2	H	B–2	M	C–2	R	D–2	W	E–2
D	A–3	I	B–3	N	C–3	S	D–3	X	E–3
E	A–4	J	B–4	O	C–4	T	D–4	Y	E–4

Checkerboard

Read the following message:

     & % & ? & % % % / ? & % % % / ?

Graf Zeppelin

What do you make of the following design:

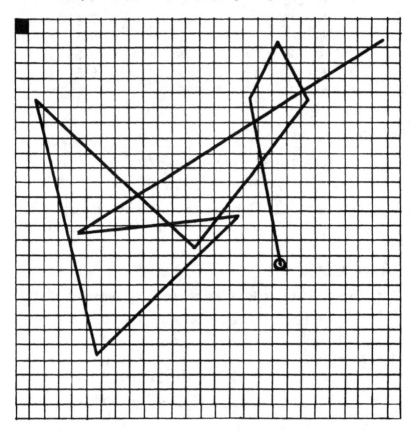

THE RANDOM KEY

"Is there really such a thing as an unbreakable code?"

Lulu asked this question very seriously to her grandfather, who was in the diplomatic service.

He smiled. "There are a good many codes that have never been broken and never will be broken. For all practical purposes, you might call them unbreakable."

"No, that isn't what I mean. I mean, is there some system that you could know, *for sure*, could not be broken?"

Her grandfather became serious. "Yes, actually there is such a cipher. It depends on a random key. You might drop all the letters in the alphabet in a box, pick out one by chance, write it down, replace the letter in the box and shake it, draw again, and so on. Then you can use this key in connection with a Vigenère table."

"And it will be really unbreakable?" she asked eagerly.

He nodded. "Yes. But of course you must observe a number of precautions. The key must be truly random (without system), it must be as long as the message to be written, and it must never be used more than once."

"But if it is so safe, then why isn't it used all the time?"

"Because there are disadvantages, too. Sometimes faster and easier codes are needed. Preparing keys, and then distributing them where they are to be used, is a long and difficult task. And then there is the possibility that spies will be able to copy the keys before they are used."

He took out a pencil and pad. "Here is a system which I call the Diplomat, because it is used in many embassies. It uses numbers instead of letters. Suppose I wanted to write the message, 'All clear.' I would copy the message, and below it copy the numbers which give each letter's position in the alphabet."

```
 A   L   L   C   L   E   A   R
01  12  12  03  12  05  01  18
```

"Now let us say that the random key we had drawn up was 15 12 03 17 25 09 16 90. You would copy the key below the other set of numbers, and add them—except that you never carry into the next column."

```
01  12  12  03  12  05  01  18
15  12  03  17  25  09  16  90
16  24  15  10  37  04  17  08
```

"The bottom line is the message that is sent. The person receiving it will copy the message, and *subtract* the random key (now with no borrowing). His answer will be changed back to letters of the alphabet, and he will have the original message."

Lulu was entranced. To think that she could use a code that the best experts in the world could not break! She had three special friends, named April, May, and June. She explained the system to them, and gave each of them a random key.

Lulu's birthday was coming soon. When her friends asked her what she wanted for a gift, she gave each of them the same message:

$$92 \quad 15 \quad 61 \quad 37 \quad 22 \quad 03$$

When her birthday arrived, Lulu opened her gifts from April, May, and June. Each gift was different, but Lulu thanked each friend warmly, and said that was exactly what she had wanted.

How do you account for the fact that Lulu got three different gifts, even though she sent her friends the same message?

Answer: Although she gave them the same message, she had not given them the same random keys. The keys were:

```
April's:   86  14  62  23  02  94
May's:     83  04  60  17  27  94
June's:    86  94  45  11  10  08
```

April read her message as follows:

```
92 15 61 37 22 03
86 14 62 23 02 94
16 01 09 14 20 19
 P  A  I  N  T  S
```

You should have little trouble figuring out what gifts May and June gave to Lulu.

THE DOUBLE HEX

By now you have become familiar with a number of methods by which a code message can be read in two different ways. It seems time to confess that there are a number of other double-meaning messages scattered through this book. Did you spot any of them?

Rabbit Farm

A message was given on page 33 reading:

```
A   L   L   Q   U   I   E   T   H   E   R   E
18  87  57  31  63  42  51  14  84  51  76  21
```

Take the first digit in each pair. If it is 1, 2, or 3, substitute 1. If it is 4, 5, or 6, substitute 2. If it is 7, 8, or 9, substitute 3.

```
1 8 5 3 6 4 5 1 8 5 7 2
1 3 2 1 2 2 2 1 3 2 3 1
```

Place three digits in a group and read, using the Thunder Mountain alphabet (page 100):

```
132 122 213 231
 H   E   L   P
```

Using a different table, the message was given:

```
A   L   L   Q   U   I   E   T   H   E   R   E
23  97  47  51  58  17  36  14  84  36  76  31
```

If the first digit in a pair is between 1 and 5, and the second digit is also between 1 and 5, place 1 below the pair. If the first digit is between 6 and 0, place 3 below the pair. Place 2 below all the remaining pairs.

```
23  97  47  51  58  17  36  14  84  36  76  31
 1   3   2   1   2   2   2   1   3   2   3   1
```

This bottom line can also be read using Thunder Mountain. The gimmick here is that the person writing the message had four choices of how to write each letter. If he chose the first choice, that gives 1; if he chose the second choice, that gives 2; if he chose the third or fourth choice, that gives 3.

Rabbit Farm II

On the table given, number the lines of the table as 1, 2, and 3 (not counting the top line). The following message was given:

SC B& TL OV O. QY CR VW MH CR YZ UV

Place three letters or symbols in a group. Below each one write the digit which tells what line that letter is on in the table. Then substitute letters, using Thunder Mountain:

SCB	&TL	OVO	.QY	CRV	WMH	CRY	ZUV
311	312	111	331	111	322	111	331
S	T	A	Y	A	W	A	Y

But as we have already seen, the supposed message, "All quiet here," already has the concealed meaning, "Help." We now have a third reading within the same message.

Gremlin Correspondence

A message was given on page 35, "Dick lost our ship's rudder at Carlton." Try reading the first letter of each word, beginning with the last word.

Gloria Scott

A message was given on page 47 beginning, "We have ever remained enthusiastic . . ." To read it in a different way from the method given, count the number of words in each sentence and substitute the corresponding letter of the alphabet:

12 5 1 22 5
L E A V E

Thunder Mountain II

Number the alphabetical lines 1, 2, and 3, on the table on page 81. Take the message and below each letter write the digit telling what line of the table it is on. Assemble these digits into groups of three's and read using Thunder Mountain:

```
S A J O Z E C Z U S O O U M E C A O WN B H G U X O & P T H
3 1 2 1 3 2 1 3 3 3 1 1 3 2 2 1 1 1 3 3 1 2 2 3 3 1 3 3 1 2
312   132   133   311   322   111   331   223   313   312
 T     H     I     S     W     A     Y     O     U     T
```

Scarab

In the solution on page 105 a message was given:

IGM WNW EKH DXX DBP VNW HVB SGO YHC KCF BDL

Take the center letter in each group, and substitute the letter immediately following in the alphabet:

G N K X B N V G H C D
H O L Y C O WH I D E

Jolly Roger

The solution on page 107 gave the following message:

D DJQ AZOKW D A DLQ AQFNO

The first letter in each group is needed to read the message in the normal way, but the remaining letters are optionals:

J Q Z O K WL Q Q F N O

Now use the following table:

	1	2	3	4	5	6	7
1	F	G	H	I	J	K	L
2	M	N	O	P	Q	R	S
3	T	U	V	WX	Y	Z	

Below each letter place the digit at the beginning of the line:

1 2 3 2 1 3 1 2 2 1 2 2

Place three digits in a group and read with Thunder Mountain:

123 213 122 122
F   L   E   E

But a third reading is also possible! Take each letter and substitute the digit above it on the table:

J Q Z O K W L Q Q F N O
5 5 7 3 6 4 7 5 5 1 2 3

Place two digits in each group, and read using Vixen:

55 73 64 75 51 23
R   E   M   A   I   N

Bacon & Eggs

Use the following table for a second reading:

1	2	3	4	5	6	7	8	9	0
A	B	C	D	E	F	G	H	I	J
N	O	P	Q	R	S	T	U	V	W

Take the message which was given and write below each letter the proper digit from the above table. Place two digits in a group and read, using Vixen:

T D C U C J W C U P D S Q Q G U J WT G
7 4 3 8 3 0 0 3 8 3 4 6 4 4 7 8 0 0 7 7
74   38   30   03   83   46   44   78   00   77
L   E   A   V   E   T   O   D   A   Y

Wrangler

	1			2			3		
	1	2	3	1	2	3	1	2	3
1	A	B	C	D	E	F	G	H	I
2	J	K	L	M	N	O	P	Q	R
3	S	T	U	V	W	X	Y	Z	&

Let's now consider a plan, not previously discussed, of putting four different meanings into the same message. Suppose we want to write the message, "We won." We can begin by using a simple cipher to bury this message into a longer message:

W____ E____ W____ O____ N____
WILL ELMER WAIT OR NOT

The two additional messages we want to bury are "Prepare" and "Do not go." We will place the Elmer message second, where it will be a little better buried, and to shorten the example we are using here, we will only write it out as far as WILL ELM:

```
P R E P A R E
W I L L E L M
D O N O T G O
```

Using Thunder Mountain, we will convert each message letter into the proper three digits:

```
2 3 1/2 3 3/1 2 2/2 3 1/1 1 1/2 3 3/1 2 2
3 2 2/1 3 3/2 1 3/2 1 3/1 2 2/2 1 3/2 2 1
1 2 1/2 2 3/2 2 2/2 2 3/3 1 2/1 3 1/2 2 3
```

Now we will use the Wrangler table shown above. The first digits from the three messages are 2, 3, and 1. Find 2 in the column to the left; our letter will be somewhere on that line. Then find 3 on the top line, and in the box immediately under it, the 1. Reading down to the second alphabetical line, our letter becomes P. 322 will give W. 121 will give D. The message reads:

P W D K Z & E K Q N T I C D E M U Y E N L

And if it so happens that PREPARE is not a true word, but a code word meaning "treasure," we have a fifth reading buried here.

This system is not really so mysterious as it seems. With Thunder Mountain, a cipher letter normally consists of three segments gathered from different parts of the message. Then why shouldn't a cipher letter be made from three segments from three separate messages?

Is there no end?

None.

The Wrangler message just given could be written right over again, using Wrangler again, and introducing two more hidden meanings. Or some other system which gives two different readings could be used. In any message, letters of the alphabet can be changed into double digits, and since there are about four times as many double numbers as there are letters of the alphabet, this means a choice is available. And where there is a choice, another reading can be hidden. Then numbers can be changed back into letters, and since there are about three times as many letters of the alphabet as there are single digits (not counting zero), this means another choice, and another opportunity to conceal a different message. Letters can be changed to numbers once more, and numbers back to letters, and . . .

A message could easily contain ten different readings. Whenever there are more letters or numbers or symbols used in the cipher message than seem to come out in the reading, there may be a different reading concealed.

Systems such as this are not highly practical, but they are fun to invent and use. And that is why you read this book.

ANSWERS TO PARTY WORD GAMES

Three-Letter Patterns

Ann, add, eke, dad, did, mom, mum
eve, inn, tee, off, fee, dud, pop, nun, ill, boo, too
gee, zoo, coo, moo, eye, bee, pup, bob, tit, tat
odd, bib, tot, egg, gag, tut, tut, pip
ewe, wee, wow, woo, pep, lee, baa
eek
eel
huh
err, gig
all, ere, ebb

Four-Letter Patterns

Otto, Anna, noon, lull, loll, yo-yo, mama, papa, peep, ooze, sass, dodo, toot, deed

Five-Letter Patterns

mommy or mammy, tepee
teeth, tooth
verve, level, eerie, sissy, nanny, rarer, llama
ninny
error, vivid
mummy, geese, sassy, mimic
booby, onion, manna, cocoa
poppy, motto, tenet, puppy or daddy

One, Two, Three

bonbon, cancan, murmur, tartar, tomtom, tsetse
beriberi

Animals

1. nightingale
2. porpoise
3. reindeer
4. rattlesnake
5. tarantula
6. terrier
7. woodpecker
8. carcass
9. caterpillar
10. cocoon
11. anteater
12. armadillo
13. baboon
14. barracuda
15. mammoth
16. bumblebee
17. chickadee
18. Chihuahua
19. chimpanzee
20. chinchilla
21. cicada
22. cockroach
23. crocodile
24. hippopotamus
25. hedgehog
26. kangaroo

ANSWERS TO PROBLEMS FOR A MATH CLASS

Einstein's Dream

Add all the digits in each group, and substitute the appropriate letter of the alphabet:

16 18 5 16 1 18 5

P R E PA R E

Watson's Needle

An IBM punch card consists of 12 horizontal rows. The top row might be called the X-row, next would come the Y-row, then the zero-row, then the one-row, the two-row, and so on until the nine-row. Numbers are indicated by merely punching out the proper digit in a particular vertical column. Letters are indicated by punching out two holes in the same vertical column. The two holes in each column which are punched for a letter are determined from the following table:

A	X–1	J	Y–1	Extra	0–1
B	X–2	K	Y–2	S	0–2
C	X–3	L	Y–3	T	0–3
D	X–4	M	Y–4	U	0–4
E	X–5	N	Y–5	V	0–5
F	X–6	O	Y–6	W	0–6
G	X–7	P	Y–7	X	0–7
H	X–8	Q	Y–8	Y	0–8
I	X–9	R	Y–9	Z	0–9

Great Caesar

The solution depends upon trying out different possible key numbers, but there are some devices to help. One way is to place the letters of the alphabet, exactly spaced, on two strips of paper, like this:

Slide the top strip into various positions over the bottom line, and try to read the message. When the correct position is located, the message will appear.

Another method is to take the message and copy the alphabet below each letter. For faster results, work toward the front of the alphabet. The original message will appear sooner or later.

```
Y H Q L Y L G L Y L F L
X G P K X K F K X K E K
W F O J W J E J W J D J
V E N I V I D I V I C I
```

Orphan Annie

The first step is to change the double-line alphabet table into a single-line table. This is accomplished by beginning with A on the top line and following it with J, the letter below. J on the top line is followed by S below. S on the top line is followed by C below. The transposed alphabet reads:

A J S C D L W O F N Z Y H Q I B K U T E M X R G P V

The next step is to take the code message and copy this transposed alphabet below each letter of the message. A clear reading will appear on some line:

```
X H T H S A R P A R N Z S O Y H G S E Y O A S X
R Q E Q C J G V J G . . .
G I M I D S P A S P . . .
P B X B L C V J C V . . .
V K R K W D A S D A . . .
A U G U O L J C L J . . .
J T P T F W S D W S . . .
S E V E N O C L O C . . .
```

If you solved this problem before seven o'clock, the universe is saved!

99

There are many ways of sliding one alphabet over another: a straight alphabet over a straight alphabet (Caesar's alphabet); a straight alphabet sliding over a transposed alphabet; a transposed alphabet sliding over a straight alphabet; a transposed alphabet sliding over the same transposed alphabet (Orphan Annie); a transposed alphabet sliding over a different transposed alphabet; 13 selected letters of the alphabet sliding over the other 13.

This system is called Orphan Annie because she used a similar system on her famous radio program. The message given each day was simple substitution, but the next day the alphabet table would be moved into a new position. But if you have broken one message, you can usually read all the others . . . if you know how!

Thunder Mountain

The entire table reads:

A	111	J	211	S	311
B	112	K	212	T	312
C	113	L	213	U	313
D	121	M	221	V	321
E	122	N	222	W	322
F	123	O	223	X	323
G	131	P	231	Y	331
H	132	Q	232	Z	332
I	133	R	233	&	333

The message was written by changing each letter into the proper three digits, then taking the first digit in the message and placing it at the end of the message, then regrouping the digits by three's, and finally substituting a letter for each group.

To read a message you must reverse these steps: change letters to digits, then take the *last* digit and place it *first*, then regroup, and finally substitute:

H Q Q D Z N E N R D Z N S Z M O E Y M N

132 232 232 121 332 222 122 222 233 121
332 222 311 332 221 223 122 331 221 222

2 132 232 232 121 332 222 122 222 233 121
332 222 311 332 221 223 122 331 221 22

213 223 223 212 133 222 212 222 223 312
133 222 231 133 222 122 312 233 122 122

L O O K I N K N O T I N P I N E T R E E

With practice, you won't have to recopy all the lines.

All that happens is that each letter is broken up into three parts, these parts are scattered and re-assembled, then changed back into letters. How many other ways can you think of to scatter and re-assemble the parts?

La Guillotine can also be used in this fashion, with each letter broken into two parts.

Thunder Mountain II

Using the preceding message (still in digit form), take the row of numbers that comes last in reading a message (first in writing a message), and regroup so there are two digits in each group:

21 32 23 22 32 12 13 32 22 21 22 22 22 33 12
13 32 22 23 11 33 22 21 22 31 22 33 12 21 22

Use Thunder Mountain II to turn these figures back into letters. 21 might be written as T, G, or S. The message might appear as:

SAJOZECZUSOOUMECAOWNBHGUXO&PTH

Pig Pen

AB	CD	EF
GH	IJ	KL
MN	OP	QR

A letter is written by drawing that portion of the diagram which goes around it. If the letter is the second letter in the box, a dot is added. The message given reads: MANY LIES.

Wigwam

Although there appear to be quite a few different symbols in this message, there are really only two. If you identify / as 1, and \ as 2, and place five digits in a group, the message can be read with Bacon's alphabet:

12222	21112	11211	12222	11111	21112	11211
P	R	E	P	A	R	E

Metric

Three symbols are used. Identify $\underline{\mathrm{I}}$ as 1; $\overline{\underline{\mathrm{I}}}$ as 2; and $\underline{\perp}$ as 3; and the message can be read using Thunder Mountain:

231	233	122	231	111	233	122
P	R	E	P	A	R	E

I. D.

A transposition cipher can be identified quite easily (unless a good many nulls—unnecessary letters—have been added) by the fact that letters such as E, T, and A will be frequent, and letters such as Q, X, and Z rare. But since this effect can be imitated, a good test is a vowel count. If about 40 per cent of the letters are vowels (including Y), it is probably a transposition cipher.

To test for simple substitution, take a letter count. A typical count may read:

17–11–10–9–6–6–6–5–5–4–4–3–3–3–2–2–2–1–1–0–0–0–0–0–0–0

This is for a 100-letter message. The letter used 17 times may very well be E, and the cipher letters representing T, A, O, and N may also be among the most common. Seven letters, probably those least commonly used, are absent. The order of letter frequencies in English is approximately as follows:

E T A O N I R S H D L M W U F C G Y P B V K X J Q Z

A Vigenère with a short key word will show a letter count less extreme than for simple substitution. A few letters will be used quite a bit more than others, and a few may be completely absent. This system is broken down by establishing the rhythm of the message. If certain letters (or combinations of letters) tend to appear five spaces apart (or a multiple of five), then there is a good chance that a five-letter key word was used. The remaining task, then, is to break down five different simple substitution alphabets and integrate the results.

If a letter count shows all letters being used approximately equally, except for what may be coincidence, then you may be faced with a Vigenère with a very long key or with an unsystematic code.

Euclid

```
P L E Y N
R O A A I
E T V D G
P E E N H
A R M O T
```

The message is read down the first column and up the second. Other ways of filling in the letters would be diagonally and in a spiral.

Although squares and rectangles are the figures used most, others are possible, such as triangles pointed in various directions, parallelograms, and trapezoids. The figure does not even need to be solid, as in the following:

```
P A
R E
E L V O N N
P O E M D O
A T     A O
R E     Y N
```

Nihilist

Cut the five messages into vertical strips. Then maneuver these slips around side by side in different positions, until you are able to spell out a message on each line. This is not nearly so difficult as it sounds. You should have no trouble completing the partial solution:

1. S O U R C E S K E P T _ _ _ _ _ _ _ _ _ _ _ _ _ _ _ _
2. D E L A Y _
3. M _
4. P _
5. P _

Model T

Chuck was referring to his code with its auto-key, or self-keying, system. Under this system, each true letter becomes the key letter in writing the following letter:

P R E P A R E T O L E A V E
X P R E P A R E T O L E A V

Now use the Rogues' Gallery to combine the pairs of letters in the manner already explained:

R X I S K H I M W X N U Z H

Many other types of keys are possible. A reference key uses a long quotation, such as Lincoln's Gettysburg Address, for a key. This breaks up the rhythm of the message.

Another type is the enciphered key, which will defeat an intercepter's attempt to find a rational key. The following example shows how the key word SPEND and the key number 1234 can be enciphered with Gremlin to produce a 20-letter key:

S P E N D S P E N D S P E N D S P E N D
1 2 3 4 1 2 3 4 1 2 3 4 1 2 3 4 1 2 3 4
T R H R E U S I O F V T F P G W Q G Q H

Any manner of enciphering a key can be used. Some ciphering

machines actually have keys that are thousands or millions of letters in length!

Scarab

One device Allan might have used was to write the first letter on the first line of the table, the second letter on the second line, and so on, and hope Ferrell could figure it out. This is the same as using the alphabet for a key.

Another device would be to write E-11, S-2, W-11, and so on. Ferrell might have been able to figure out that he was to start with Q in the upper lefthand corner of the table and go east 11 spaces, from there south two spaces, and so on.

A third device would be to take a piece of transparent paper and lay it over the Rogues' Gallery table, select the first letter of his message anywhere in the table, select the second letter and draw a line to it, and so on. This transparent paper would be sent to Ferrell, who might be able to figure out he is supposed to lay it on top of his copy of the table.

The device Allan actually used was to find each letter in the body of the table, and substitute the *two* letters which would give the row and the column. Taking these two letters, Ferrell would find where they intersect on the table, and that would be his real letter.   A message might read:

```
M   I    S   S   B   I    G   W   A   N   T   S   E   S   S   A   Y
IG  GM  WN  NW  EK  KH  DX  XX  DB  BP  VN  NW  HV  VB  SG  GO  YH

            T   O   D   A   Y
           HC  KC  CF  BD  DL
```

To illustrate an entirely different point, if the cipher letters are placed four in a group, the second and third letters of that group are the same. The repeated letter can be dropped for a case where three cipher letters equal two real letters:

IGM WNW EKH DXX DBP VNW HVB SGO YHC KCF BDL

The middle letter joins with the preceding letter as well as with the following letter to produce two true letters.

Vampire

With this system, if a letter appears on the first line, simply substitute the digit above. But if it appears on the second or third line, substitute the digit at the beginning of the line *and* the digit above. A word might be written:

P R E P A R E
73 9 21 73 6 9 21

If this bottom line is now run together, the opposition will have trouble figuring out that one digit stands for one letter, except that 2 and 7 never stand alone but always need an additional digit.

Gregg

These messages were written in Gregg shorthand, and read:

1. I would like a piece of apple cake.
2. This system is very different from ours.
3. It will be good to see you again.

Of course a stenographer would not write letters of the alphabet, but would write the equivalent shorthand symbols instead.

Noah's Ark

The message reads, "Can you come with me Saturday?" It was written by looking up each word in the dictionary, and substituting the third word after it. Now that you know how it was done, try another:

Weakling arena unassuming toast megrim theodolite pride

Valley of Fear

Some codes use the idea of looking up a word in a book and substituting page, line, and word number. Because of the difficulty of locating the words needed in a book, a dictionary, which has the words ordered alphabetically, is often used for this purpose. The table shows on what page each letter of the alphabet begins in a 1000-page dictionary. From the numbers in the message, it is possible to find the first letter in each word, and this offers an excellent start in breaking the code.

Vixen

Did you notice that the clue sentence contains all the letters of the alphabet? This makes it useful for secret messages. It can be written into a form of Rabbit Farm:

	1	2	3	4	5	6	7	8	9	0
1	T	H	E	Q	U	I	C	K	B	R
2	O	W	N	F	O	X	J	U	M	P
3	S	O	V	E	R	T	H	E	L	A
4	Z	Y	D	O	G	T	H	E	Q	U
5	I	C	K	B	R	O	W	N	F	O
6	X	J	U	M	P	S	O	V	E	R
7	T	H	E	L	A	Z	Y	D	O	G
8	T	H	E	Q	U	I	C	K	B	R
9	O	W	N	F	O	X	J	U	M	P
0	S	O	V	E	R	T	H	E	L	A

The message is now easily read: HOLD FAST.

Bacon & Eggs

If a letter is in the first half of the alphabet, put a 1 below; if it is in the second half of the alphabet, put a 2 below. Then read with Bacon's alphabet:

TDCUC JWCUP DSQQG UJWTG
21121 12122 12221 21221
  S   L   O   W

Jolly Roger

The first step is to space the message correctly. Make a break before every A, B, C, D, and E:

D DJQ AZOKW D A DLQ AQFNO

Count only the first letter in each group, and follow it with the number of letters remaining in the group. Then use the alphabet table to read the message:

D–0 D–2 A–4 D–0 A–0 D–2 A–4
 P   R   E   P   A   R   E

Checkerboard

Four different symbols appear in the message, which leads to the suspicion that there are really five symbols (the fifth did not happen to appear in this short message). Proceeding on this guess, place two symbols in a group:

&% &? &% %% /? &% %% /?

Place a 1 under the first group, and under any other group with the same two symbols. Place a 2 under the second group, 3 under the fourth group, and so on:

1 2 1 3 4 1 3 4

Now refer to your list of fingerprinted words, and find: NONSENSE.

Graf Zeppelin

Write the alphabet in the line across the top, and also in the column to the left. Begin with the circled dot. This gives PR. Move on to the next dot, which gives EP. The third dot gives AR, and so on.

INDEX